The Triune Identity

God According to the Gospel

The Triune Identity

ROBERT W. JENSON

FORTRESS PRESS   PHILADELPHIA

Library of Congress Cataloging in Publication Data

Jenson, Robert W.
  The triune identity.

  Includes bibliographic references and index.
  1. Trinity. I. Title.
  BT111.2.J46   231'.044   81–43091
  ISBN 0–8006–0672–8   AACR2

36,501

9026K81   Printed in the United States of America   1–672

IN MEMORIAM VIRI ORNATISSIMI
PETER BRUNNER
† DIE XXIV MENSIS MAII IN ANNO MCMLXXXI DOMINI
DOCTORIS CONFESSORISQUE FIDEI
MEI IN THEOLOGICIS PATRIS
ET AMICI VENERABILIS

Contents

Preface

It need not be argued that the Western church now little uses or understands Christianity's heritage of trinitarian reflection and language. So long as Christianity was the established religion of the West, the Western church could just barely survive this debility. The doctrine of the Trinity comprises, as we shall see, the Christian faith's repertoire of ways of *identifying* its God,[1] to say *which* of the many candidates for godhead we mean when we say, for example, "God is loving" or "Dear God, please. . . ." So long as we could suppose it obvious which putative god would truly be God if there were any, Western Christians could shut their eyes to the disuse of these means. We no longer have that luxury. In the foreseeable future the life of the Western world will be very like that of the declining Mediterranean antiquity in which Christian trinitarian language was first created—presenting a different divine offering on every street corner. For Christian discourse to be intelligible, we shall have to accept our place as one item of this pluralism and make clear—first and principally to ourselves—*which* god we mean, before we venture his reality or characteristics. Therefore the Western church must now either renew its trinitarian consciousness or experience increasing impotence and confusion.

Here we only note that during the time of the Western church's religious establishment and shelter, trinitarian insight and discourse in fact declined; explanation will occupy us later. The trinitarian heritage includes sophisticated metaphysical dialectics with which the greatest thinkers of Christian history explored the truth of their God, perhaps more deeply than the thinkers of any other religious tradition. Most Christians—lay, professional, or clerical—now know nothing of such matters. In the best—or worst—case they say that God is both one and three, as a sheer paradox they are supposed to believe because it is "revealed." The trinitarian heritage includes the triune rhetorical and dramatic structure of Christian liturgy, but this structure is vital in few service books and fewer congregations. Even the triune pattern of the Supper's Great Thanksgiving is lost in most Western orders, including the Roman canon and some of its current replacements, and efforts to restore the pattern have for centuries met with incomprehension. Fundamental in the trinitarian heritage is the triune proper name of Christianity's particular God: "Father, Son, and Holy Spirit." The mere use of the phrase as a name—to say nothing of understanding why it is so used—has now little place in believers' piety. Currently people are offended with the name for a variety of irrelevant reasons, and their random proposals to replace it with, say, "Ground, Logos, and Spirit" or "Parent, Child, and Spirit" meet little cogent resistance. Finally and centrally, the trinitarian heritage includes the dogma decreed at Nicaea and Constantinople. It is little evoked in congregations or seminaries, and much of what is said is historically wrong and long known to be wrong.

After such a lament I might well be asked, Why not give up trinitarianism? Many think we should. Those most shaped by the centuries of Christianity's establishment, and therefore most uncritically sure that "of course everyone really worships the same God," regularly propose to meet pluralism just that way.[2] Since we can no longer avoid noting that human groups identify their gods differently and irreconcilably, they propose to save their assumption by denying that God has any identity and by holding that all specifications—such as the church's trinitarian language—of *which* is God are of merely preliminary value. The move is plausible, but it will not do.

A theology and religion of no-god-in-particular or all-gods-at-once would be religiously vacuous and intellectually uninteresting, for the big theological words—"saving," "loving," "awesome," and so on—share a logical peculiarity:[3] they are so dependent on analogy and suggestion that they constantly threaten to lose all cognitive function. Predicated merely of "some god," they do just that. "X redeems," for example, is not an ordinary open sentence making a specific assertion about an unspecified subject, for until "X" is specified we do not in fact know what "redeems" says about her/him/it. Only if we replace "X" with, for example, "Baal," does "redeems" acquire the cognitively functioning—possibly true or false—sense "sends rain." Prior to identification of God, or subsequent to all identifications' transcending, all that "X redeems" can mean is "X restores whatever state X defines as good"—which leaves us religiously just where we were. More generally, without identification of God, all that can be said about her/him/it is "God is the object of ultimate concern," or something of the sort—which is of analytical importance but which advances us religiously only when we are told which concerns are right and reasonable, that is, which possible God is real.

It is possible to miss these simple points only because of a logical quirk. It is precisely the specificity of some particular gods, the "Absolutes" of high Indian religion or Neoplatonism, that they have only negative characteristics, so that each is in fact identified as "the—very specifically—Unidentifiable One." Thus it is easy to suppose one is affirming all-gods-in-general without religious vacuity when one is in fact affirming the specific God of sophisticated India or Alexandria and benefiting from India's or Alexandria's specific religious inheritance. But that this blunder in logic is easy and common does not make it respectable.

In a religiously plural age the question of God's identity recovers its natural primacy. The question *whether* God is, is the vital question when asked about a particular putative God. Asked in the form "Is there any god at all?" it is a religious and intellectual triviality. Only when we specify *who* or *which* allegedly is God is "God is" a threat or a promise, a solution or a conundrum. And the question *what* God is *like* is itself a request for either God's identification or further information about a God already identified. Humankind cries out: *Where* may we turn? To *whom* may we pray? *What* power may we invoke? By *what name*? Christianity answers: We may pray to Jesus' "Father," whom in his Spirit we too may address as Father. Those who suppose Christianity to be true, and therefore wish to answer so, must in our time relearn the answer's depths and subtleties; that is, they must relearn—and carry further—trinitarian piety and thought.

As already presumed in the foregoing, the doctrine of the Trinity is no one doctrine or homogeneous set of doctrines, such as is, for example, the Anselmian doctrine of atonement. There are several kinds of trinitarian discourse, each of which functions differently within the church's effort to identify its God. Sorting them out is one of the clarifications I hope to offer readers of this book, because confusion between them has perhaps been a major barrier to understanding.

Throughout the book, I have two different but inseparable aims: (1) to make the trinitarian tradition lucid—which does not mean easy—and (2) to develop proposals for its reform and further development. It belongs to the nature of theology that these two aims cannot be neatly sorted out. Readers should be aware that my report of the tradition, while as accurate as I could make it, is not systematically neutral. It is not offered as a replacement for the standard historical summaries—though naturally I hope it improves on them (and whether they are systematically neutral is another matter). Thus the very division into chapters, with its particular classification of "sorts of trinitarian discourse," is already one of this book's main constructive proposals.

In the trinitarian inheritance, we find—I propose—first God's proper name: "Father, Son, and Holy Spirit." That this is so, that this phrase and its variants in fact have functioned and do function as a proper name, and that it is to perform this function that the phrase appears is in my opinion a true statement about the tradition and is shown to be true by Chapter 1's presentation of aspects of the tradition. But so far as I know, previous theology has not explicitly said that "Father, Son, and Holy Spirit" is a proper name, nor therefore drawn some of the interesting consequences of this fact, though many, especially Karl Barth, have come close to making the observation and have affirmed positions that are in fact the observation's consequences.

In Chapter 2, I have analyzed the tradition's first-level trinitarianism, the trinitarianism of speech habits and liturgies and immediate interpretation of experience, as embodying a primal Christian logic and rhetoric. This seems the right way to analyze this aspect of the inheritance. But readers should keep in mind that the proposal to achieve understanding in just this way is an innovation, for better or worse.

The division of Chapters 3, 4, and 5 is more usual, although even here it is not common to make as definite a distinction as I do between the dogmatic statement of Christianity's trinitarian identification of God and dialectical analysis of this identification. My pervasive use in these chapters—as in the first two—of the concept of identity, both as a means of understanding the tradition and as a means of reforming and extending it, is in my opinion fair to the tradition but is not itself traditional. In general, of course, it is in these chapters that my own critique of traditional formulations and my own materially constructive proposals are thickest on the ground.

The double purpose of the book has resulted in some literary asymmetries which I hope will not mislead readers. Some sections are dauntingly footnoted, others sparsely; this does not reflect greater and lesser study or reflection. Chapters discussing traditional developments that seem to me much in need of explanation and sorting out are longer than chapters that can go more directly to the present point; differing bulk of the exposition should not be taken to represent differing importance of the matter. Finally, the very great historical and reflective range that I have tried to cover means that I know less than I need to at some places; without spending my life on this book, that could not be fully rectified.

Acknowledgments

For the achievement of this work, I owe thanks to several persons and institutions. I thank Blanche, as always. I thank Gettysburg Seminary for a sabbatical during which much new reading was done, and the Aid Association for Lutherans and the Lutheran Church in America for financial assistance. I thank Union Seminary in New York City for use of their fine library. And I thank the director of Fortress Press, Norman Hjelm, for extraordinary support.

NOTES

1. Barth made this clear. See Karl Barth, *Kirchliche Dogmatik* (Zurich: Zollikon, 1932–67), 1:339ff.

2. E.g., John Hick, *God and the Universe of Faiths* (New York: Macmillan, 1973).

3. E.g., Antony Flew and Alasdair MacIntyre, eds., *New Essays in Philosophical Theology* (London: SCM, 1955).

Abbreviations

The abbreviations used in this book, as given below, are based on Siegfried Schwertner, *International Glossary of Abbreviations for Theology and Related Subjects* (Berlin and New York: Walter de Gruyter, 1974).

AThANT Abhandlungen zur Theologie des Alten und Neuen Testaments

CChr.SL *Corpus Christianorum*. Latin Series. Turnholt, 1953ff.

CP *Classical Philology*.

DThC *Dictionnaire de théologie catholique*. Paris, 1903ff.

EnchP *Enchiridion patristicum*. Edited by Marie Joseph Rouët de Journel. Freiburg, 1911, 1959.

EvTh *Evangelische Theologie*.

JThS *Journal of Theological Studies*.

KEK Kritisch-exegetischer Kommentar über das Neue Testament.

KuD *Kerygma und Dogma*. Göttingen, 1955ff.

PG *Patrologiae cursus completus*. Greek Series. Edited by Jacques-Paul Migne. Paris, 1857–66, 1928–36.

RGG³ *Die Religion in Geschichte und Gegenwart*. Tübingen, 1909ff.

SJTh *Scottish Journal of Theology*.

StNT Studien zum Neuen Testament.

TaS Texts and Studies. Contribution to Biblical and Patristic Literature. Cambridge, 1891–1952, 1954ff.

ThWNT *Theologisches Wörterbuch zum Neuen Testament*. Edited by Gerhard Kittel. Stuttgart, 1933ff.

VT.S *Vetus Testamentum. Supplement*. Leiden, 1953ff.

WA Luther, Martin. *Werke. Kritische Gesamtausgabe*. Weimar, 1883ff.

ZKG *Zeitschrift für Kirchengeschichte*.

ZThK *Zeitschrift für Theologie und Kirche*.

1

"Father, Son, and Holy Spirit"

The Sense of "God"

What *can* be said prior to God's identification must be said. What do people use this word "God" for, that we ask so urgently to whom or to what it is truly applied?

The horizon of life and its concerns is time, the inescapable no-more, still, and not-yet of all we know and will. That this is so is indubitable and can be confirmed also from those religions and metaphysical systems that posit life's fulfillment in escape from time. The observation that it is so, on the other hand, is perhaps not so universal and is a contribution of the two great contradictory interpretations of reality: that of the Hebrew and Christian Scriptures, which embrace time, and that of high Indian religion, which seeks to abolish it.

Every human act moves from what was to what is to be: It is carried and filled by tradition but intends new creation. Just so our acts hang between past and future, to be in fact temporal, to be the self-transcendence, the inherent and inevitable adventure, that is the theme of all Western religion and philosophy. But just so also, our acts threaten to fall between past and future, to become boring or fantastic or both, and all life threatens to become an unplotted sequence of merely causally joined events that happen to befall an actually impersonal entity, "me."

Human life is possible—or in recent jargon "meaningful"— only if past and future are somehow bracketed, only if their disconnection is somehow transcended, only if our lives somehow cohere to make a story. Life in time is possible only, that is, if there is "eternity," if no-more, still, and not-yet do not

1

exhaust the structure of reality. Thus, in all we do we seek eternity. If our seeking becomes explicit, we practice "religion." And if our religion perceives the bracket around time as in any way a particular something, as in any way the possible subject or object of verbs—as in, for example, "The eternal speaks by the prophets"—we tend to say "God" instead of "the eternal."

But already we are becoming intolerably indefinite, for manifestly there are many kinds of bracketing that can be imagined around past and future, many possible eternities. There is, for example, the eternity of tribal ancestors who have become so old that nothing can surprise them any more and in whose continuing presence all the future's putative novelties are therefore mastered by traditional maxims. There is the eternity of Nirvana, where a difference of past and future is just not permitted. There is the eternity of existentialism, in which sheer decision brings time momentarily to a halt. And so on. So multiform is eternity that the mere assertion that it is, that there is *some* union of past and future, that life has *some* meaning, is for practice as good as the suspicion that there is none at all. Life is enabled not by a posit *that* life means, but by a posit of *what* it means. The plot and energy of life are determined by *which* eternity we rely upon, and the truth of any mode of life is determined by the reality of the eternity it posits. If we speak of "God," a life's substance is given by which God we worship, and a life's truth is given by whether this is the God that really is.

Pondering the foundation of biblical faith, the Exodus, Israel's first theologians made Moses' decisive question be: "If I come to the people of Israel and say to them, 'The God of your fathers has sent me to you,' and they ask me, 'What is his name?' what shall I say to them?" If Israel was to risk the future of this God, to leave secure political nonexistence in Egypt and venture on his promises, Israel had first and fundamentally to know which future this was. The God answered: "Say this to the people of Israel, [Yahweh], the God of your fathers, the God of Abraham, the God of Isaac, and the God of Jacob, has sent me to you; this is my name for ever, and thus I am to be remembered through all generations" (Exod. 3:13–15).[1]

The answer provides a proper name, "Yahweh." It also provides what logicians call an identifying description, a descriptive phrase or clause, or set of them, that fits just the one individual entity to be identified. Here the description is "the God whom Abraham and Isaac and Jacob worshiped." The more usual description is that found in a parallel account a few chapters later: God said to Moses, "Say . . . to the people of Israel, 'I am [Yahweh], and I will bring you out from under the burdens of the Egyptians . . . ; and you shall know that I am [Yahweh], *who* has brought you out. . . . I am [Yahweh]'" (Exod. 6:2–7).

In general, proper names work only if such identifying descriptions are at hand. We may say, "Mary is coming to dinner," and be answered with, "Who is Mary?" Then we must be able to say, "Mary is *the one who* lives in apartment 2C, and is always so cheerful, and . . . ," continuing until the questioner says, "Oh, *that* one!" We may say, "Yahweh always forgives," and be answered with, "Do you mean the Inner Self?" Then we must be able to say, "No. We mean the one who rescued Israel from Egypt, and. . . ."

Linguistic means of identification—proper names, identifying descriptions, or both—are a necessity of religion. Prayers, like other requests and praises, must be *addressed*. Thus the typical prayer-form of Western Christianity, the collect, usually begins with an identifying description such as, "O God, *who* didst give thine only-begotten Son to be. . . ." The moral will of God must be proclaimed as a particular will if we are to follow it. Paul set a pattern for Christian preaching when he wrote to the Philippians: "Have *this* mind among yourselves, *which* is yours in Christ Jesus, *who* . . ." (Phil. 2:1–11). Eschatological promise must be specified; proclamation of a final union of mankind is gospel because the gathering is to be around the risen Jesus, but it would be quite something else were the gathering to be around a risen Stalin.

Trinitarian discourse is Christianity's effort to identify the God who has claimed us. The doctrine of the Trinity comprises both a proper name, "Father, Son, and Holy Spirit," in several grammatical variants, and an elaborate development and analysis of corresponding identifying descriptions.

One more step of this preliminary analysis may be taken. In that an eternity is always some union of past and future, every possible eternity will be of one of two broad kinds: a Persistence of the Beginning, or an Anticipation of the End.[2] Moreover, essential time is future time. It is because we face a future that we experience ourselves as temporal beings; if there were only the past, which remains forever as it is, we would be timeless. The eternity in which all persists as it was is therefore the cancellation of time; the eternity in which all is open to transformation is the success of time itself.

Therefore religion is either refuge from time or confidence in it. God may be God because in him all that will be is already realized, so that the novelties of the future are only apparent and its threats therefore not overwhelming. Or God may be God because in him all that has been is opened to transformation, so that the guilts of the past and immobilities of the present are rightly to be interpreted as opportunities of creation. God may be our defense against time's uncertainties, or he may be himself the "Insecurity of the future."[3] Brahman-Atman, by any of his names, may be God, in which case all time is illusion, circling around a blissful utter Sameness. Or Yahweh may be God, in which case all sameness will be overcome by the God who makes all things new, whose very righteousness is his love of sinners, of those who are lost if the past determines. It is the consistent exemplifications of these opposite possibilities that make history's two great religious worlds.

If, as seems to be the case and as our rhetoric has already suggested, deity of the future is historically exemplified only once, by the God of Israel, classification of gods by the directions of time turns out itself to be projected by believing insight. This need not mean that the classification does other religions an injustice, or even that any of them could not accept it, only that the horizon of time is not the first they would mention to particularize themselves. Even here, there is no escape from particularity, nor any reason to want it.

We live in the present; that is tautology. But the content of present life is memory and expectation, in some union. We speak of "God" to name that union. Or rather, we speak to and from God to invoke it. Just so, we need to know who he is, to know how our lives hang together. Trinitarian discourse is Christianity's answer to this need. The first part of the answer is a name.

Israel's Identification of God

What the word "Yahweh" may once have meant we do not know. Since historical Israel did not know either, the loss is not theologically great. "Yahweh" was for Israel a pure proper name which no doubt had once been applied on account of its sense but had survived the knowledge thereof.[4] Indeed, in the famous passage in which Moses asks for an explanation of the name, Yahweh is depicted as replying with a play on an ad hoc etymology precisely to reject such curiosity: "I am who I am" (Exod. 3:14).[5]

It is remarkable that "Yahweh," with its variants, was the *only* proper name in ordinary use for Israel's God; other substantives, predominantly "Elohim," were used as common terms and appellatives.[6] Other ancient peoples piled up divine names;[7] the comprehensiveness of a god's authority was achieved by blurring his particularity, by identification of initially distinct numina with one another, leading to a grandly vague deity-in-general. Israel made the opposite move. Israel's salvation depended precisely on unambiguous identification of her God over against the generality of the numinous. In the Yahwistic account of Yahweh's decisive self-revelation at Mount Sinai, the central passage is: "And [Yahweh] descended . . . and proclaimed the name [Yahweh] . . . : '[Yahweh, Yahweh], a God merciful and gracious'" (Exod. 34:5–6), which is precisely what gods in general could not be. Therefore it was included in Israel's fundamental description of righteousness, the Ten Commandments, that Israel must not demean the name of Yahweh (Exod. 20:7).

So decisive in Israel is the identifying proper name that the Priestly tradition, extending from the Pentateuch through Ezekiel and Second Isaiah, can make the knowledge that "I am [Yahweh]" be the whole fruit of God's acts in Israel.[8] God's judgments are for this purpose: "I will punish you for your ways. . . . Then you will know that I am [Yahweh]" (Ezek. 7:4). And so is his mercy: "I will establish my covenant with you, and you shall know that I am [Yahweh]" (Ezek. 16:62). God introduces himself, and this event is salvation: "I am [Yahweh], your God, the Holy One of Israel, your Savior. . . . Fear not, for I am with you. . . . I, I am [Yahweh], and besides me there is no savior. . . . I, I am He who blots out your transgressions for my own sake" (Isa. 43:3–25).

A proper place for prayer, sacrifice, or consultation of the oracles was therefore one where the name "Yahweh" was known (Exod. 20:24). What happens at such a holy place can be compendiously described as "calling on the name [Yahweh]" (Gen. 12:8; 13:4; etc.). Blessings are "applications" of the name Yahweh (Num. 6:27; Deut. 10:8; etc.), and prayers are addressed by it (e.g., 1 Kings 18:24). The worshipers' use of "Yahweh" is their reason for confidence that their offering will be acceptable and their petitions heard, for those who know God's name are his people, to whom he has committed himself (Ps. 20:1–3; 25:11). And when God did not want to be grasped, he withheld his name (Gen. 32:30); the heathen are heathen just because they do not know it (Ps. 79:6).

To go with the name, Israel had identifying descriptions. At the very foundation of Israel's life, the introduction to the basic Torah of the Ten Commandments, the two are neatly side by side: "I am [Yahweh], your God, who brought you out of the land of Egypt" (Exod. 20:2). There were, of course, many descriptions that could be used to identify Yahweh, but this one, the narrative of Exodus, was that on which Israel's faith hung.[9] The Exodus was the chief content of Israel's creed: "And you shall make response before [Yahweh] your God, 'A wandering

Aramean was my father; and he went down into Egypt. . . . And the Egyptians treated us harshly and afflicted us. . . . Then we cried to [Yahweh] . . . , and [Yahweh] brought us out of Egypt with a mighty hand . . . and he brought us into this place and gave us this land'" (Deut. 26:5–9; see also Josh. 24:1ff.). The entire narrative of the Hebrew Scriptures is an expanded version of the creedal narrative just cited.[10] And the whole Torah was understood as explication of the Exodus' consequences: "You have seen what I did to the Egyptians, and how I . . . brought you to myself. Now therefore . . ." (Exod. 19:4–5). To the question "Whom do you mean, 'God'?" Israel answered, "Whoever got us out of Egypt."

In the Bible the name of God and the narration of his works thus belong together. The descriptions that make the name work are items of the narrative. And conversely, identifying God, backing up the name, is the very function of the biblical narrative. A passage in Ezekiel begins, "On the day when I chose Israel, I swore to the seed of . . . Jacob, making myself known to them in the land of Egypt . . . , saying, I am [Yahweh] your God. On that day I swore to them that I would bring them out of the land of Egypt." There follows a long version of the narrative creed—or short version of the Pentateuch. The passage ends, "I did it that they might know that I am [Yahweh]" (Ezek. 20:5–26).

The act of calling God by name was in Israel so tremendous that, as the identification of the true God over against other claimants ceased to be a daily challenge, and use of the name therefore ceased to be a daily necessity, actual pronunciation of the name ceased, at least for all but the mightiest occasions.[11] This is reflected in the pointing of YHWH in our Hebrew text with the vocal points for "Adonai," "Lord," as a signal to speak this word instead, and in the Septuagint translation of "Yahweh" by "Kyrios."

Identifying God in the New Testament

The gospel of the New Testament is the provision of a new identifying description for this same God; that this new description comes to apply is the event witness to which is the whole point of the New Testament. The content of the gospel is that God can now be known as "whoever raised Jesus from the dead."[12]

Identification of God by the resurrection did not replace identification by the Exodus, for it is essential to the God who raised Jesus that he is the same who freed Israel. But the new thing that is the content of the gospel is that God has now identified himself also as "him that raised from the dead Jesus our Lord" (Rom. 4:24). In the New Testament such phrases therefore become the standard way of referring to God.[13]

Theologians sometimes fall into futile disputes about whether the crucifixion or the resurrection—or something else—is most important, and New Testament exegetes are sometimes so impressed by the conceptual variety and propositional disagreement they find among the various traditions that they deny any theological consistency in the New Testament. Such blunders are the result of failing to sort out differing conceptual functions. If we say, "God is good," and wish to explicate the predicate "good" there are a variety of paths open, in the course of which we may refer to the resurrection, the crucifixion, the life of Jesus, or items from the Hebrew Scriptures. But if we are asked instead about the *subject*, "Which God do you mean?" there are no New Testament answers other than "the God of Israel"—which gets us back to the Exodus—or "him who raised Jesus." On the other hand, the resurrection itself can appear as a predicate, as in "Jesus rose." If now "rose" is to be explicated, various paths again open. And if Jesus—not, now, God—needs to be identified, this will be done with items of his biography. The resurrection is thus the logical hinge of New Testament specific theology.[14] But that is the matter of Chapter 2.

To go with this new identifying description there are not so much new names as new kinds of naming. "Yahweh" does not reappear as a name in use; the habit of instead saying "Lord" has buried it too deeply under the appellative.[15] But in the church's missionary reality, actual use of a proper name in speaking of God is again necessary in a variety of contexts. It is the naming of Jesus exclusively that occurs for all such functions. Exorcism, healing, and indeed good works generally are accomplished "in Jesus' name"; church discipline and quasi-discipline are carried out by sentences pronounced "in Jesus' name"; and forgiveness is pronounced in the same way. Baptism is described as "into Jesus' name," whether or not it was ever actually performed with this formula, and undergoing such baptism is equated with that calling on the name "Yahweh" by which, according to Joel 3:5, Israel is to be saved. Above all, perhaps, prayer is "in Jesus' name," in consequence of which the name can be posited as the very object of faith. Believers just *are* "those who call on the name of our Lord Jesus Christ."[16]

So dominant was the use of the name "Jesus" in the religious life of the apostolic church that the whole mission can be described as proclamation "in his name," "preach[ing] the good news about the kingdom of God and about the name of Jesus Christ," indeed as "carrying" Jesus' name to the people (Luke 24:47; Acts 4:17–18; 8:12; 9:15). The gatherings of the congregations can be described as "giving thanks . . . in the name of our Lord Jesus Christ," indeed, simply as meetings "in" his name (Eph. 5:20; Matt. 18:20). Where faith must be confessed over against the hostility of society, this is "confession of the name" (Mark 13:13 and par.; Matt. 10:22; Luke 21:12; John 15:21; Acts 9:16; 1 Pet. 4:14ff.). The theological conclusion was drawn in such praises as the hymn preserved in Philippians in which God's own eschatological triumph is evoked as cosmic obeisance to the name of "Jesus," or in such formulas as that in Acts which makes Jesus' name the agent of salvation (Phil. 1:10; Acts 4:12). However various groups in the primal church may have conceived Jesus' relation to God, "Jesus" was the way they all invoked God.

One other new naming appears in the New Testament, the triune name, "Father, Son, and Holy Spirit." Its appearance is undoubtedly dependent on that invoking of God by naming Jesus which was just discussed, but the causal connections are probably no longer recoverable. It is of course this name toward which we have been steering. That the biblical God must have some proper name, we have seen in the Hebrew Scriptures. In the life of the primal church, God is in fact named by uses that involve the name of Jesus. "Father, Son, and Spirit" is the naming of this sort that historically triumphed.

The Triune Name

That "Father, Son, and Holy Spirit" in fact occupies in the church the place occupied in Israel by "Yahweh" even hasty observation of the church's life must discover.[17] Why it came to be so is the matter of the next chapter; for now we merely register the fact. Our services begin and are punctuated with "In the name of the 'Father, Son, and Holy Spirit,'" and our prayers conclude, "In his name who with you and the Holy Spirit is . . ."; above all, the act by which persons are brought both into the fellowship of believers and into their fellowship with God is an initiation "into the name 'Father, Son, and Holy Spirit.'"

The phenomenon we are here concerned with is the use of such threefold phrases also when the argument or conceptual framework does not suggest it. To take as an example one of the earliest documentations, before 110 A.D., Ignatius of Antioch, in a context of *dualist* rhetoric and reflection nevertheless uses the *triple* name when he mentions God. Christians, he says, are to strive for perfection "in the flesh and in the spirit, in faith and in love, in the Son and the Father and the Spirit, in the beginning and in the end."[18] It is the speech habit that is to be noted; believers have habitually used the triple phrases also when there is no special reason to do so, that is, they have used them as a proper name.

The habit of trinitarian naming is universal through the life of the church. How far back it goes we cannot make out. It certainly goes further back than even the faintest traces of trinitarian reflection, and it appears to have been an immediate reflex of believers' experience of God. It is in liturgy, when we do not talk about God but to and for him, that we need and use his name, and that is where the trinitarian formulas appear, both initially and to this day.

The trinitarian formulas' first appearances in surviving literature are all glimpses of the earliest church's liturgical life. The passage just quoted from Ignatius is liturgical divine *law*, which calls God to judge; so are another passage in Ignatius and two of three passages in the letter of Clement to Corinth.[19] The third appearance in Clement is an *oath:* "As God lives, and as the Lord Jesus Christ lives, and the Holy Spirit. . . ."[20] In so-called 2 *Clement* there is a trinitarian *benediction.*[21] And in the *Martyrdom of Polycarp* a magnificent *doxology*, of a form still in daily liturgical use, is put in the mouth of the dying martyr: "I glorify you, through the eternal heavenly High Priest, Jesus Christ, your beloved Child, through whom be glory to you with him and the Holy Spirit."[22]

In the immediately postapostolic literature there is no use of a trinitarian formula as a piece of theology or in such fashion as to depend upon antecedent development in theology, yet the formula is there. Its home is in the liturgy, in baptism and the Eucharist, and there its use was regularly seen as the heart of the matter.[23] Thus, for example, in the East Syrian church a trinitarian invocation at the Fraction was seen as the main consecratory event:[24] "Bread . . . we name the name of the Father over thee; we name the name of the Son over thee; we name the name of the Spirit over thee—the exalted name that is hidden from all."[25]

There are two New Testament occurrences of a trinitarian naming-formula. The earliest is the closing benediction of Paul's second letter to Corinth (2 Cor. 13:14). The epistolary benedictions of the New Testament reflect epistolary custom, liturgy, and, no doubt, personal style. They occur in the opening salutations and at the closing. If we sort them out, there is a surprising result. The opening benedictions all name both "God the Father" and "the Lord Jesus Christ." The closing benedictions—with one exception—either name no one and are simple wishes of "grace," or name only the Lord Jesus. Moreover, the naming of the Lord Jesus occurs in all and only the authentic letters of Paul and is obviously his idiosyncrasy. Then suddenly, in one Pauline letter, and that neither the earliest nor the latest, a trinitarian naming replaces the naming of the Lord Jesus only: "The grace of the Lord Jesus Christ and the love of God and the fellowship of the Holy Spirit be with you all."

These circumstances prohibit all thought of development from one-membered to two-membered to three-membered formulas.[26] So far as the texts let us see, all forms are equally immediate, the choice depending on custom and chance. The particular trinitarian formula that ends 2 Corinthians looks like Paul's creation of the moment, apropos of nothing special in the letter, and done only because it was natural to do. The purely christological benediction that was Paul's habit—"The grace of our Lord Jesus Christ be with you"—expands in both directions by its own logic. Or if Paul did not create this greeting here, he took it from liturgical use in the same unmotivated and obvious fashion.

The most important New Testament trinitarian naming is the Matthean baptismal commission (Matt. 28:19). Baptism is the church's chief sacrament, its rite of passage from old reality to new.[27] Within such a rite, the new reality must be identified, for the neophytes must be directed into it. In baptism, as often in initiation rites of other religions, this is done by naming the God whose reality it is. The name stipulated in the canonical rubric for baptismal liturgy is "Father, Son, and Holy Spirit."[28]

It is often supposed that the tripartite baptismal formula developed from unitary or bipartite formulas: "In Jesus' name" or "In the name of God and of the Lord Jesus." There is indeed evidence from the second century of baptism with such formulas; as to an origin of the trinitarian formula from these, however, it may have been so, but there is no evidence.[29] In any case, the tripartite formula was soon there, and it is the only one in the New Testament.

The triune name did not, of course, fall from heaven; it was made by believers for the God with whom we have found ourselves involved. "Father" was Jesus' peculiar address to the particular Transcendence over against whom he lived.[30] Just by this address he qualified himself as "the Son," and in the memory of the primal church his acclamation as "Son" was the beginning of faith.[31] "Spirit" was the term provided by the whole biblical theology for what comes of such a meeting between this God and one to whom he takes a special relation. It is involvement in this structure of Jesus' own event—prayer to "Father" with "the Son" in the power of and for "the Spirit"—that is faith's knowledge of God. Thus "Father, Son, and Holy Spirit" summarizes faith's apprehension of God; this is the matter of the next chapter. But in the event so summarizable, "Father, Son, and Holy Spirit" came together also simply as a name for the one therein apprehended, and it apparently did so before all analysis of its suitability. That the triune name is itself composed of names is a specific structure of this suitability, and also a matter of the next chapter, but here we should note that on the first occasion where "the Trinity" appeared as a short replacement of the triple formula, around 180 A.D., it too appeared as a name.[32]

One further matter must be discussed here: the masculinity of "Father." Emerging consciousness of the historic oppression of women rightly watches for expressions thereof also, or perhaps principally, in inherited interpretation of God. When such are found, Christianity has every reason to eliminate them, and we will in fact find a decisive area where male sexism has shaped the structure of doctrine. Trinitarian "Father"-language cannot, however, be another, and the widely spread supposition that it is another is a breakdown of linguistic and doctrinal information and sophistication.[33]

The church's trinitarian naming incorporates and results from Jesus' filial address to God. That Jesus in fact called God "Abba," which can only be translated "Father," must settle the matter for trinitarian naming, since as we have noted and will analyze at length, it is Jesus' historical reality that makes the name work. But of course, that we may not substitute for "Father" in the triune name may mean only that the whole name is irremediably offensive. And the use of "Father" within the trinitarian name cannot be altogether separated from its more general use in Christian speech to and about God.

For filial address to God the choice of words is limited, for us as for Jesus. "Parent" and its natural or artificial equivalents cannot be regular filial terms of address because they do not individuate. That leaves "mother" and "father." It is decisive for Israel's God that his filial relation to us is established only by his sheer will, that is, that his role as our parent is not sexual, that he is not even metaphorically a fertility God.[34] It is decisive also for the inner-trinitarian parent-child relation—to anticipate discussion of these relations—that the parenting involved is not a cooperative enterprise between a begetter and a bearer, that there is only one parent, not two. To posit such a cooperative work within the divine would be not trinitarianism but polytheism. By both considerations, therefore, the choice between "Mother" and "Father," as terms of filial address to God, was and must be made according to which term is more easily separable from its function as the name of a role in our bisexual reproduction.

Sexuality, as the union of sensuality and differentiated reproductive roles and apparatus, is the glory of our specific humanity. It is the way in which our directness *to* each other, both among those now living and between generations—and that precisely by differences between us—is built into our bodies, into our sheer created givenness. Moreover, within the mutuality of male and female, the female is ontologically superior. She is the more ineradicably human, for while sensuality and reproduction can be ripped apart in the male, by alienating economic or political structures or by personal abnegation or incapacity, so that sexuality is undone, not even generally available abortion can do this to the female—short, of course, of the "brave new world" or of humankind's decision to die out.

Therefore in religions where the direct religious analogy from human perfections to divine characteristics is undisturbed, the female gender has been religiously dominant, even in otherwise male-dominated societies. That the gender identification of the gods reflects gender dominance within societies is simply not the case; male-dominated societies are as likely as female-dominated ones to have predominantly female deities.[35] The swaggering lords of the Achaean military states worshiped mostly Hera, Athena, and Artemis, the overlordship of Zeus coming later. The chief divine gender will be female when just two conditions are fulfilled: when a society has an integral relation to the given (Christians say "created") structures of human life and when deity is grasped by projection onto eternity of the values established in those structures.

Thus, one way in which predominant divine femaleness may be broken is by alienation from the givens of our existence. This alienation may be mere chaos and confusion, or it may be deliberate, attendant on a transition from modes of life controlled by biological rhythms to modes chosen and characterized by "free" choice, as in classical Athens and Sparta and in the world civilization taught by them.[36] Here the attribution of maleness to dominant deity will have actual sexual content, just as in the opposite situation it replaces. It is this sort of male divinity that can have no place in Christianity and must be overcome when discovered.

But matriarchy within deity may also be broken in a different way, which can happen also when the relation to creation is integral and which does not replace divine femaleness with divine maleness but rather abolishes the whole attribution of sexuality to deity. Israel was not permitted to grasp God's ways by ours, and specifically not to grasp God's creativity by ours; thus her God was understood to be sexually transcendent. Therefore, in Israel when a filial term of address is needed it is the ontological inferiority of the male, the fragility of his sexuality, that offers "Father" rather than "Mother" as the proper term of address. That the biblical God is sexually transcendent does not, of course, mean that he is less than sexual, but rather that what we are by sexual differentiation he is without the various relations of more and less which sexual differentiation indeed involves. That Jesus, and we after him, have called God "Father"—or, indeed, "he"—thus involves no valuing of masculinity above femininity. On the contrary, it is the only available way to satisfy the determination of Israel and the church to attribute neither to God. As for "Father and

Mother," which incredibly has actually been used in services wishing to be Christian, it is most objectionable of all, since by insisting on both it makes the attribution of sexual roles entirely inescapable and repristinates the deepest fertility myth, that of divine androgyny. The biblical God is not *both* our begetter and our bearer. He is *neither*.

The assumption that it is a deprivation not to address God in one's very own gender is a case of humankind's general religious assumption of direct analogy from human perfections to divine qualities. In the faith of the Bible, this direct line is, for our salvation, broken. Indeed, Christianity's entire soteriological message can be put so: God's self-identification with the Crucified One frees us from having to find God by projection of our own perfections. Therefore no argument that depends on the assumption of unbroken analogy from human worth to divine characteristic can have any place in the church.

All speech about God is of course, in a commonsensical way, by analogy. But the gospel is free to take its analogies sometimes from human perfections and sometimes from human imperfections, depending on theological need. Sometimes it takes them from death and sin, by no means thereby ranking these above life and virtue. It can even take them from fatherhood— saying thereby nothing whatever about the relative worth of fatherhood and motherhood.

The Name as Doctrine

So far we have merely noted a historically contingent fact about the church's discourse. Now we must note that it is a fact with authority, in view of the biblical stipulation of the triune name for baptism.[37] The impact of this dogma extends far beyond the baptismal rite itself.[38] The function of naming God in initiation, in baptism as elsewhere, is to address the initiate to new reality, to grant new access to God. In the community of the baptized, therefore, the divine name spoken in baptism is established as that by which the community has its particular address to God.[39]

It has in fact worked out so in the church, both liturgically and theologically. In the church's life of prayer and blessing, threefold invocation is established at every decisive point. And in the theological history we will tell in a following chapter, we will find the role of the baptismal formula so predominant that there would be reason to call "Go . . . baptizing in the name of the Father and of the Son and of the Holy Spirit" the founding doctrine of the faith.

From time to time, various concerns lead to proposed replacements of the trinitarian name, for example, "In the name of God: Creator, Redeemer, and Sanctifier" or "In the name of God the Ground and God the Logos and God the Spirit." All such parodies disrupt the faith's self-identity at the level of its primal and least-reflected historicity.

Such attempts presuppose that we first know about a triune God and then look about for a form of words to address him, when in fact it is the other way around. Moreover, "Creator, Redeemer, and Sanctifier," for example, is, like other such phrases, not a name at all. It is rather an assemblage of after-the-fact theological abstractions, useful in their place but not here. Such assemblages cannot even be *made* into names, for they do not identify. Every putative deity must claim, for example, somehow to "create," "redeem," and "sanctify." There are also, to be sure, numerous candidates to be "Father" or "Spirit," but within the trinitarian name, "the Father" is not primarily *our* Father, but the Father of the immediately next-named Son, that is, of Jesus. The "Holy Spirit," within the name, is not merely any "spirit" claiming to be holy, but the communal spirit of the just-named Jesus and his Father. By these relations *inside the phrase,* "Father, Son, and Holy Spirit" is historically specific and can be what liturgy and devotion— and at its base, all theology—must have, a proper name of God.

The ancient church, which first understood the necessity of trinitarianism, was well aware of these distinctions. There is a passage in Athanasius too illuminating not to repeat. The Arians made just such an abstraction as "Ground"—in their case, "The Unoriginate"—into the sole identifying description of

God. Athanasius grants the usefulness of such theological abstractions in various analytical and even proclamatory contexts.
But: ". . . 'Father' was made known to us by our Lord . . . ,
who knew whose Son he is. . . . When he taught us to pray
he did not say 'When you pray, say "O God Unoriginate . . . ,"'
but rather "Our Father. . . ."' And he did not call us to baptize
'in the name of the Unoriginate and the Originate . . .'
but 'in the name of the Father and the Son and the Holy Spirit.
. . .' Those who name God 'Unoriginate' name him only from
his external works . . . ; but those who name God 'Father'
immediately signify in him also the Son . . . , naming him from
the intimate issue of his own being. . . ."[40]

The last remarks again claim that "Father, Son, and Holy
Spirit" is not an arbitrary label. A proper name is proper just
insofar as it is used independently of aptness to the one
named, but it need not therefore lack such aptness. "Father,
Son, and Holy Spirit" is appropriate to name the gospel's God
because the phrase immediately summarizes the primal Christian interpretation of God. It is this second level of trinitarianism to which we must now turn.

NOTES

1. The knotty matter of whether such a phrase as "God of Jacob"
was once a proper name is outside our concern; in this context "the
God of your fathers" is clearly descriptive.

Brackets around "Yahweh" (Hebrew: YHWH or JHWH) are used
throughout this book in quotations from the Revised Standard Version of the Bible. The RSV follows the Jewish custom of avoiding the
proper name of God and substituting "the Lord," but in this book
we are speaking precisely of God's proper name and thus use the
name "Yahweh."

2. This analysis has been a chief preoccupation of modern the-
ology and will be in this book. It should be noted that an Eternal
Now does not make a third possibility; it is the same as the Eternal
Past.

3. Rudolf Bultmann's famous slogan.

4. Gerhard von Rad, *Theologie des alten Testaments* (Munich: C.
Kaiser, 1957–65), 1:20–21.

5. Walther Zimmerli, *Old Testament Theology in Outline*, trans. D. E. Green (Atlanta: John Knox, 1978), pp. 19–20.

6. Von Rad, *Theologie*, 2:187–88.

7. Ibid., p. 186.

8. Walther Zimmerli, "Ich bin Jahveh," in his *Gottes Offenbarung* (Munich: C. Kaiser, 1963), pp. 11–40.

9. Zimmerli, *Theology*, pp. 21–27.

10. Von Rad, *Theologie*, 1:127ff.

11. From the third century B.C., see K. Baltzer, "Namenglaube im alten Testament," *RGG*³ 4:1302–4.

12. See recently Peter Stuhlmacher, "Das Bekenntnis zur Aufwerweckung Jesus von den Toten und die biblische Theologie," *ZThK* 70 (1973): 365–403, esp. pp. 377–91.

13. Cf. Rom. 4:24 with Rom. 8:11; 1 Cor. 15:15; 2 Cor. 1:9; 1 Pet. 1:21.

14. See Stuhlmacher, "Das Bekenntnis."

15. As a name, "Kyrios" appears only in Scripture references, e.g., Matt. 4:10; 22:37. Otherwise, referring to God, it is only an alternate to "Theos."

16. Matt. 7:22 and pars.; Mark 9:37ff.; 16:17; Luke 10:17; John 1:12; 14:13–14; 15:16; Acts 2:21, 38; 3:6; 9:14; 10:43; 22:16; Rom. 10:9–13; 1 Cor. 1:1; 1:10, 11–13; 2 Thess. 3:6; James 5:10; 1 John 2:12; 3:25.

17. See Josef A. Jungmann, *The Place of Christ in Liturgical Prayer*, trans. A. Peeler (New York: Alba House, 1965).

18. Ignatius *Letter to the Magnesians* 13.1.

19. Ibid., 13.2; Clement *To the Corinthians* 42.3; 46.6.

20. Clement *Corinthians* 58.2.

21. *2 Clement* 20.5.

22. *Martyrdom of Polycarp* 14.3.

23. Georg Kretschmar, *Studien zur frühchristlichen Trinitätstheologie* (Tübingen: J. C. B. Mohr, 1956), pp. 182–216, has established this from liturgical evidence.

24. Ibid., pp. 191–96.

25. *Acts of Thomas* in *New Testament Apocryphal Books*, ed. William Wright (Amsterdam: Philo, 1968; reprint of 1871 London ed.), p. 268.

26. Such as is posited by Henry A. Wolfson, *The Philosophy of the Church Fathers* (Cambridge: Harvard, 1956), 1:147–54.

27. Robert W. Jenson, *Visible Words* (Philadelphia: Fortress Press, 1978), pp. 126ff.

28. As far back as Christian liturgical practice can be traced, invocation of "the Name," usually trinitarian, is seen as the chief

agency of baptism's power to transform, even in the West, where the triple name appears in the form of questions. See Kretschmar, *Studien*, pp. 135–216.

29. The passages in Acts that describe baptism "in Jesus' name" (2:36; 8:16; 10:48; 19:15) are all theological descriptions, not rubrics. For second- and third-century practice, see ibid., pp. 196–216.

30. E.g., Günther Bornkamm, *Jesus of Nazareth*, trans. I. and F. McLuskey (New York: Harper & Row, 1960), pp. 124–29.

31. Martin Hengel, *The Son of God*, trans. J. Bowden (Philadelphia: Fortress Press, 1976).

32. Theophilus of Antioch *Apology to Autolycus* 2.15. The Latin *trinitas* was a neologism to translate *trias*.

33. Driven to exasperation by the Arians' habit of pressing every divine epithet to the unimaginative end, Gregory Nazianzus once exploded: "Probably you could be foolish enough to suppose our God male . . . because the word is? Or the Spirit neuter because he neither begets nor bears? Or even that God cohabited with his own Will (grammatically feminine in Greek), according to the old myths, to beget the Son—which posits the androgynous God of Marcus and Valentinus?" (*Orations* 31.7). Whatever may have been true of the Arians, it is to be feared that some moderns are at least that linguistically naive.

34. Von Rad, *Theologie*, 1:24ff.

35. See, e.g., the kind of material in Martin P. Nilsson, "Die Griechen," in *Lehrbuch der Religionsgeschichte*, ed. Chantepie de la Saussaye (Tübingen: J. C. B. Mohr, 1929), 2:306–27.

36. E.g., Ulrich Mann, *Vorspiel des Heils* (Stuttgart: Klett, 1962), pp. 16–31, 46–158.

37. Cf. Jenson, *Visible Words*, pp. 6–11.

38. For an account of the spread of the baptismal formula into the rest of the primal church's worship, see Kretschmar, *Studien*, pp. 182–216, esp. p. 195.

39. See Basil the Great *On the Holy Spirit*, in *PG* 32:67–218; Gregory of Nyssa *Refutation of Eunomius' Confession*, in his *Opera*, vol. 2, ed. W. Jaeger (Leiden: Brill, 1952), p. 313.

40. See Athanasius *Epistle on the Decrees of Nicaea* 31; *Discourse Against the Arians I*, 34; and *Letter to Serapion* 4–6.

2

The Trinitarian Logic and Experience

The Trinitarian Logic

"Father, Son, and Holy Spirit" became the church's name for its God because it packs into one phrase the content and logic of this God's identifying descriptions. These in turn embody the church's primal experience of God. In turning from the trinitarian name to the logic and history by which it became the name, we therefore also move out from the church's specific life of praise and petition, in which a name is most needed, to the wider whole of the church's life and reflection.

The gospel identifies its God thus: God is the one who raised Israel's Jesus from the dead. The whole task of theology can be described as the unpacking of this sentence in various ways. One of these produces the church's trinitarian language and thought.

If for any reason we attend to the temporality of "God is whoever raised Jesus," we note certain temporal features, which have been noticed, at least liturgically, from the church's very beginning. God is here identified by a narrative that uses the tense-structure of ordinary language, whereas divine identification is more ordinarily done by time-neutral characters, as in "God is whoever is omnipotent to bolster my weakness" or "God is whatever is immune to the time which takes away my life." If this narrative were mythic, there would still be nothing out of the way, for the tenses would not be used in their ordinary way and the tense-structure of ordinary language would still not shape our interpretation of God. But the narrative is not mythic, for it depends for its power to identify on mention of a historical individual and so, in turn, on the historical nar-

21

rative by which he must be identified. Such a procedure is religiously peculiar, as has often been noticed, usually with offense, for while religions often mention some historical event—a "revelation"—as epistemologically necessary for their knowledge *about* God, they do not normally *identify* the *subject* of this knowledge by that event.

To identify the gospel's God, we must identify Jesus. In this sense we may first say that God "is" Jesus. Every reality is somehow identifiable, and we cannot identify this God without simultaneously identifying Jesus. This also displays why religions do not normally pin their identifications of God to the identity of a historical event, for drastic restrictions are imposed on the ways in which we can go on to talk of a God so identified. If God, in *any* sense, *is* Jesus—or were Abraham Lincoln or the British Empire—we cannot rightly talk of this God in any way which would make the temporal sequences, the stuff of narration, unessential to his being, and that, of course, is just how religions normally want to talk of God. Indeed, the posit of one to whom tenses are insignificant and in whom, therefore, time may be evaded is the whole usual point of their enterprise.

God, we may therefore identify, is what happens with Jesus. But if we said only that, we would show no reason why it should be *God* that happens with Jesus and not merely, perhaps, an important religious epoch. Moreover, it is not as if we in any case knew about God and then for some reason decided to "identify" him by reference to Jesus. It is rather what in particular happens with Jesus that compels us to use the word "God" of *this* "Father" in the first place.

Following much of the New Testament, let us use "love" as a slogan for what humanly happened with the historical Jesus. Then we may say that Jesus was a lover who went to death rather than qualify his self-giving to others; the love which was the plot of his life is an unconditional love. Of this person it is said that he nevertheless lives, that he is risen. Said of this particular person, such an assertion—whether true or not—is appropriate, for love means an unconditional self-giving and an acceptance of death, and a successful love would be an acceptance of death which nevertheless did not result in the lover's absence from the beloved, but in his presence. Love must finally *mean* death and resurrection. For this particular man, resurrection, if it happened, was therefore but the proper outcome of his life.

And if this lover's resurrection happened, then there also now lives an unconditional lover with death—the limit of love—already behind him, so that his love must finally triumph altogether, must embrace all people and all circumstances of their lives. If he is risen, the human enterprise has a conclusion: a human communion constituted in its commonality by one man's unconditional self-dedication to his fellows, and so embracing each individual and communal freedom established in the history so fulfilled.

Thus, if Jesus is risen his personal love will be the last Outcome of the human enterprise. If he died, his self-definition has been written to its end, as each of ours will be, but if he also nevertheless lives, just this life so defined is not thereby a dead item of the past but an item of living, surprising time, an item of the future and indeed of the last future. Only of a person whose life had been defined as this particular man defined his would these propositions be appropriate. And it is because they are appropriate, and in that they are in fact made, that "God" is an appropriate word for the reality identifiable as what happened with Jesus. For a God is always some sort of eternity, some sort of embrace around time, within which time's sequences can be coherent, and if Jesus is risen he is to be both remembered and awaited.

Conversely, we may identify God so, now a second time: God is what will *come* of Jesus and us, together. In our original proposition, "God is whoever raised Jesus," the event by which God is identified—Jesus' resurrection—is the event in which Jesus is future to himself and to us.

In the Bible generally, the "Spirit" is God as the power of the future to overturn what already is, and just so fulfill it. The Spirit is indeed a present reality. But *what* is present is that there is a Goal and that we therein are free from all bondage to what is. The Spirit is the power of the Eschaton now to be at once Goal and Negation of what is. In the New Testament, this Spirit is identified as Jesus' spirit, as every person has spirit. That Jesus' particular spirit is the very power of the last future is the "Spirit"-form of the identification of God by Jesus from which trinitarian language begins. Therefore the biblical "Spirit" is the inevitable word for this second identification of God, although developed trinitarian doctrines, since they respond to postbiblical problems, need by no means be bound exclusively to this name.

Finally, this particular embrace around time must be universal, for it is the embrace of an unconditional love. It must grant a universal destiny. Therefore this God may also be identified thus: God is the will in which all things have Jesus' love as their destiny. Jesus, we say, "is" God only *as* God's identifiability. In our original identifying proposition, "God is whoever raised Jesus," "Jesus" is the object of an active verb. God is—a third time—identified as the one who *does* Jesus' resurrection, as a *given* active Transcendence to all that Jesus is and does. As what happens with Jesus is its own and our End, so also it is its own and our Given.

In the New Testament, "Father" is Jesus' address to the Transcendence *given to* his acts and sufferings, the Transcendence *over against* whom he lives and to whom he is responsible—addressed in trust. For Jesus' disciples, therefore, "the Father" is God as the transcendent Givenness of Jesus' love, the one in whom we may trust for that love.

Thus we have a temporally three-point identification of the gospel's God. If we think of an identification as a pointing operation—as in "Which one?" "That one"—we must point with all three of time's arrows in order to point out this God: to the Father as Given, to the Lord Jesus as the present Possibility of God's reality for us, to the Spirit as the Outcome of Jesus' work. The identification is triple—rather than, say, double or quintuple—because time does have three arrows. The past, present, and future of all that is, is doubtless a peculiar sort of fact but also the most inescapable.

That the gospel's identification of God is threefold rests, therefore, on the way the gospel modulates a generally available and inescapable metaphysical fact. What is peculiar about the gospel's identification of God is not the number three but rather that it follows the three arrows of time without mitigating their difference. It is the very purpose of most discourse about gods to mitigate the threatening difference of past, present, and future. Among us Greeks, this is ordinarily accomplished by a doctrine of God's being as a timeless Persistence in which past, present, and future are "really" all the same. The gospel's theology cannot produce such a doctrine, for thereby it would saw off the limb of narrative identification on which all its talk of God sits. But if such a doctrine is not produced, we are left with the three peculiar Christian identifications of God and with their even more peculiar mutual relation.

The God of the gospel is the Hope at the beginning of all things, in which we and all things are open to our fulfillment; he is the love which will be that Fulfillment; and he is the Faithfulness of Jesus the Israelite, which within time's sequences reconciles this Beginning and this End. All else being equal, nothing more need be said. The temporal structure we have analyzed is the open horizon of the church's unreflected life and proclamation. Trinitarian discourse becomes problematic, and the difficult metaphysical dialectics we will shortly have to work through become necessary only when mitigation of time becomes tempting, that is, only in confrontation with more normal identifications of God. The confrontation of that sort which historically occurred is the matter of the following chapter.

The Soteriological Necessity of Trinitarian Logic

We may make the same point soteriologically. Then we will say: For salvation's sake, Christian doctrine of God may not seek to transcend revelation in time and confront God "himself" beyond time. But only by such transcending of the temporal revelation would we reach a "real" God beyond the three.

All religions posit revelation, for all agree that if God were knowable in the same way as pencils or galaxies, there would not be God. But just in that revelations are necessarily events or objects in time, religion that seeks a time*less* eternity must at its highest level of achievement and consciousness leave its revelation behind, as "initial truth" or "outward symbol." Just that is what faith in the gospel can never wish to do.

It cannot because the gospel is an *unconditional* promise of Fulfillment. The gospel does not merely launch a quest, upon the success of which salvation must then depend. It does not say, "If you follow the path that is here revealed, you will find fulfillment." It says rather, "Because Jesus, who has bound himself to you unto death, lives with death behind him, you will surely be fulfilled." Therefore, either the gospel is the last word from God, the object of *final* reliance, from which there is no call to move on to higher things, or it is false. "Do not say . . . , 'Who will ascend into heaven?' (that is, to bring Christ down). . . . The word is near you, on your lips and in your heart (that is, the word of faith which we preach) . . ." (Rom. 10:6–8). Asked "Show us the Father," the Johannine Jesus does not respond, "If you look hard, in such-and-such a way, you will find him." He says rather, "You have seen me; therefore you have seen the Father" (John 14:8–11).

It is just this primal gospel-apprehension—that there is no way or need of getting to God past what happens with Jesus in time, so that the temporal structure of that event must be left as ultimate in God—that has moved all the great trinitarian teachers of the church. Thus Gregory of Nyssa: "He whose curiosity rises above the Sun passes also by the thought of the Father"; for such, ". . . faith is . . . vain, the message empty, baptism pointless, and the pains of the martyrs for nothing."[1] What is at stake is nothing less than whether our talk of God is truly to be of God and to be a *saving* talk of God. The slightest departure from the trinitarian logic must either trivialize our apprehension of God, replacing him with one or another convenient godlet, or plunge us into a confrontation with God that will destroy us. Of the teachers of the church, no other has understood this with such clarity as Martin Luther, and I must record his teaching here, at the beginning of this book, to secure both the necessity and the object of all that follows in it.[2]

By Luther's drastic insight, we may not seek to rise above the temporal revelation of God, thinking to grasp God more truly, in his high majesty, because the true God's majesty is precisely his hiddenness, his refusal to be grasped by any but himself. We can honor and obey the divine majesty of God "in himself" only by refraining from the religious quest for God "in himself" beyond his temporal revelation, only by truly obeying the Socratic motto "Quae supra nos, nihil ad nos" (What is above us is none of our business).

In describing God's deity as hiddenness, Luther in one way continues an ancient theological tradition of identifying God's deity by "invisibility," "intangibility," "ineffability," and so on, a tradition which we will later find much cause to criticize. But Luther also breaks the tradition. He describes God not with mere negatives but with the active "hides himself." God is not hidden from us by mere metaphysical distance, so that if we do get a little way toward him he will be less hidden; God is hidden precisely by his ineluctable nearness to us. The true— that is, biblical—God, Luther knew, is a storm blowing all creatures before himself, an unquenchable Will closer to each creature than the creature is to itself. In his sheer deity, God works all in all without discrimination: good and evil, life and death, creation and destruction. Just so he is hidden, his purposes untraceable, his reasonings inscrutable, his character opaque. The only real God is the God within whose will all things occur; just so, given what in fact occurs, he is a moral enigma, beyond—or below?—good and evil, a Terror in the night. Every attempt to approach him must either erect some protective image of the divine, that is, some idol, between him and us, or end in despair. And the apprehension that God works all in all and just so hides himself is not itself a piece of theologizing independent of the gospel about Christ. It is precisely the unconditionality of the gospel that makes us see God so, for if

God can promise unconditionally the Fulfillment of all history, and if we can trust his promises, clearly no events can be beyond his control. "If you doubt . . . that God foreknows and wills all things . . . , necessarily and immutably, how will you be able . . . to rely on his promises?"[3] And it is exactly the revelation of God in Jesus' crucifixion and resurrection, as unconditional love, that makes God who works all in this world where so little love appears, who "seems . . . to delight in the tortures of the wretched and to be more worthy of hate than of love,"[4] an impenetrable enigma. Precisely by revealing himself God hides himself, repelling our religious quest to grasp him.

So also God's self-revelation in Christ is not itself an abandonment or mitigation of his hiddenness, for since his hiddenness is his deity, such a revelation could only present us with another godlet, another of the depotentiated divinities of our religiosity. Rather, God reveals himself by hiding yet again, by exercising his very deity, but by now hiding under the opposites of all that sheer omnipotence which hides him and is his mere deity, under weakness and forgiveness and death. He defines his hiddenness, and thus he makes it speakable and speaks it, as the hiddenness of love.

Thus both as the hidden God and as the revealed God, the one God directs us away from himself as we might seek to grasp him "above" his human life and cross and resurrection, toward himself as he defines himself for us in these events of our own time and history. Just and only so, he is true God and one God, and any attempt by us to execute the opposite movement can only either create a God who is indeed all too plainly only *our* God or dash us against the true God where he is not ours.

Trinitarian Life

The trinitarian logic just analyzed is not an abstract possibility; it is the structure of the church's historical existence, as authoritatively described in the New Testament. We see this in both fundamental churchly realities: the mission and the Lord's Supper.

At the very beginning there was no difference between the church and its mission; the first gatherings of believers were gatherings of missionaries.[5] The Christian mission had, so far as we can see, two roots. One was Jesus' sending of his disciples, during his historical career, to proclaim throughout Israel the imminence of the Kingdom (Mark 6:6–13 pars.; Luke 10:1–12; Matt. 9:37–38; 10:5–16).[6] This mission was neither a matter of merely informing the people nor a search for converts in the modern sense; it was itself an integral event of the Kingdom's advent. The disciples are the "harvesters" (Matt. 9:37–38), as in the parables the angels are, who carry out the eschatological gathering of the Lord's folk.[7]

The crucifixion seemed to terminate and refute this mission. But with the resurrection, Jesus' message and sending were confirmed and then given ultimate urgency, for now the End was actually in progress.[8] Thus the Matthean and (pseudo)-Marcan mission-commands of the risen Lord reproduce the vocabulary of the earlier sending of the disciples: "Go . . . and preach" (Matt. 16:15; Mark 21:19; Matt. 10:6–7).[9] Israel had to be turned toward its coming Lord; the believers were to be the messengers.

The mission's other root was Israel's expectation of salvation for all nations. It early became clear to Israel that her God must be the God of all peoples and that his saving will must therefore somehow embrace them (Gen. 12:3; Ps. 82). In the proclamation of the great prophets and with increasing force through the Exile, the eschatological consequences are drawn. It is the very role of Israel to be a witness to *all* nations for the true God, not by going out to make converts but simply by her own faithfulness.[10] When Israel becomes the true witness, all peoples will be united around her in the one true God and his love and justice: "It shall come to pass in the latter days that the mountain of the house of [Yahweh] shall be established as the highest of the mountains . . . , and all the nations shall flow to it . . . and say: 'Come, let us go up to the mountain of [Yahweh] . . . , that he may teach us his ways. . . .' For out of Zion shall go forth the law and the word of [Yahweh] from Jerusalem. . . . And they shall beat their swords into plowshares . . . , neither shall they learn war any more" (Isa. 2:2–4; also Mic. 4:1–4; Isa. 45:18–25; 60:1–22).

At the very beginning of the church all but the "Judaizers" understood that the resurrection, as the beginning of the End, meant that the way was now open to the gentiles.[11] The differences concerned what this meant for the mission. Some evidently maintained a modified apocalyptic schedule of coming events. The believers' mission to Israel is one thing, the gathering of the gentiles in principle God's act thereafter; nevertheless, since the barriers are fundamentally fallen, when the mission to Israel also touches gentiles they too are to be baptized and received (Acts 10:1—11:24). But others, in the sweep of the last days, saw no remaining sequence of coming events, but only the Lord's one advent; thus the mission to Israel and God's gathering of the nations can be but one event: ". . . and you shall be my witnesses in Jerusalem and in all Judea and Samaria and to the end of the earth" (Acts 1:8). It is apparent that if the first group at all recognizes the second (the "Apostolic Council"; Gal. 2:1–10; Acts 15:1–19), the second must soon dominate. The Christian church was created by a mission that saw itself, and was carried out, as God's own eschatological act to unite humankind.

The theology of this mission is compendiously stated in the Matthean mission-command (Matt. 28:18–20). The basis is eschatological and christological. The risen Messiah is already now enthroned in God's omnipotence: "All authority in heaven and on earth has been given to me."[12] The worldwide preaching of the gospel, the going of the disciples to "all nations," is an exercise of this power. It can be such an exercise because in it the Lord himself is present: "And . . . I am with you . . . to the close of the age."

It should not be seen as merely coincidental that the rubric for baptism contained in this sending stipulates the triune name, for the mission itself, as here commanded, is triune. The one who speaks and sends and is proclaimed is the present risen Lord. But he does not simply *have* his power; it has been given to him—there is one over against whom he lives and from whom he has his omnipotence. As to the power he has and gives, this is eschatological power, power at "the close of the age," to which other documents of the same tradition give the name: "You shall receive power when the Holy Spirit has come upon you" (Acts 1:8; see also Luke 24:49; Mark 16:17–18). This eschatological power is in turn identical with the presence of the Lord himself: "I am with you." And finally, though the pericope is theologically packed and in the present composition is the product of deep reflection,[13] there is no trace of any attempt to locate "real deity" more in one of these temporal dimensions than in another.

The Christian missionary lives in the trinitarian time-pattern. Blown onward by the Spirit, he serves the Lord to carry out the promises of the Father.[14] And he does not mitigate the tension of his situation, that is, he does not compromise these instances in any timeless unity.

For a second object of analysis, we turn from the church's outward direction to the heart of its internal life, the Thanksgiving at the Supper. So obtrusive is the necessary triune pattern of this rite that it became in fact one of the chief supports of later trinitarian doctrinal development. The origins of the Supper are too complex to discuss here. However it came about, by the time Paul wrote to Corinth it was already authoritative tradition that we are to "do this, for my remembrance" (1 Cor. 11:24–25; Luke 22:19). Whether this canonical rubric is taken as a historical word of the Lord or as a gloss on the whole text, emphasizing its character as rubrical instructions for congregations' practice, makes no final difference. Either way, "Do this" specifies "Give thanks," coming together in the thanksgiving by sharing a loaf and a loving-cup.[15]

As to the character of the mandated thanksgiving, we are well instructed about such Jewish table-thanksgiving. So, evidently, was the earliest church, for primal Christian practice was exactly what modern scholarship would derive from the biblical mandate. Indeed, the pattern of the ancient prayers seems to have been determined by direct development from Jewish forms.[16] Moreover, this pattern was for centuries well maintained in the ecumenical tradition.

The root utterance of Jewish table-thanksgiving is "Blessed

be the Lord God!"[17] The content of this praise is then developed by giving its reasons, God's saving past acts, for example,
"who has given us a good and spacious land." Thus the *praise*
of God is accomplished by *remembrance* of his temporal action.
And within eschatological faith this remembering necessarily
fulfills itself in *invocation* of those acts of God yet to come, to
which his past acts commit him, for example, "May he mer-
cifully find us worthy of the day of Messiah and of the life to
come." In rich variation, this temporal structure is the form of
all Jewish praise, especially of the table-thanksgivings.

In addition, the canonical rubric for *Christian* thanksgiving
stipulates two specific characteristics. First, when we remember God's acts, we are to include centrally what happened with
Jesus: "Do this, for *my* remembrance" (Luke 22:19; 1 Cor.
11:24–25).[18] Second, eschatological invocation is to be central
and specific; at our Supper we "proclaim the Lord's death *until
he comes*" (1 Cor. 11:26). It only remains to give the New Testament name, "Spirit," to the power of such eschatological
anticipation, to have the explicit trinitarian structure: we praise
the Father, for remembrance of the Son, with invocation of the
Spirit.

So obtrusive is this structure that in the most ancient church
the Thanksgiving was often understood as an act *of* the Trinity:
as praise to the Father, offered *with* the Son and the Spirit. So
the Thanksgiving of Serapion: "May the Lord Jesus speak in
us, and the Holy Spirit, and may they praise you through us.
For you are above all power and principalities."[19] The conception is found in Justin, Irenaeus, and a variety of lesser
sources.[20] In consequence, the entire Thanksgiving, as conse-
cration, could be interpreted as a trinitarian naming in analogy
to baptism;[21] for Origen, the host was "bread over which the
name of God and Christ and the Holy Spirit is named."[22]

As the standard orders of Christian Supper-Thanksgiving
developed, the trinitarian deep structure determined also the
outward succession of items.[23] Throughout the ecumenical tradition,[24] from the fourth century on, the Supper's Thanksgiving opens with the explicit praise of God the Father, reciting
some selection of his mighty works in Creation, in the history

of Israel, and conclusively in the death and resurrection of Christ. In most orders, this christological narration leads smoothly into the "narrative of institution,"[25] a remembering of the particular act in Christ by which our Supper itself is justified. Following this long "first article" section, there is the "anamnesis," the explicit attempt to obey the command that our Thanksgiving shall be for Jesus' remembrance. The matter of this part will best be stated by quoting the classic example of the first *Book of Common Prayer*: "Wherefore, O Lord . . . , we . . . do celebrate, and make here before thy divine Majesty, with these thy holy gifts, the memorial which thy son hath willed us to make, having in remembrance his blessed passion, mighty resurrection, and glorious ascension, rendering unto thee most hearty thanks for innumerable benefits bestowed unto us by the same. . . ." It will be noted how much the narrative content of this section is like that of the second article of a trinitarian creed. Finally, there is the "epiclesis," the invocation of the Spirit and of the future the Spirit brings, stretching to the eschaton, for example, the ordinary epiclesis of the *Lutheran Book of Worship*, "Send now, we pray, your Holy Spirit . . . , that we . . . may live to the praise of your glory and receive our inheritance with all your saints in light."

From the beginning and to this day, the congregation gathered at the Supper gives trinitarian thanks to God. He is praised as the giver and doer of all good. The good that he does is Christ. And of that good will come the final good, present and anticipated in the Spirit. Thereby, the congregation shares the very triune life of God.

The Hebrew Scriptures as Root
of Trinitarianism

There is a famous saying of an anonymous first-century preacher that we must "think about Jesus Christ as we do about God."[26] The dictum formulated a principle that was immediate and self-understood through the apostolic and immediately postapostolic time,[27] for to think of God in the *way* this chapter has so far analyzed *is* to think of Christ as of God.[28]

Whether such thinking remains immediate and obvious or

is difficult and problematic, and so also whether we just *do* such thinking or also reflect on what we do, depends of course on how one does in fact antecedently think about God. As the Hebrew Scriptures, and so the earliest church, think of God, there is no problem, and none was felt. As the religion and philosophy of the Greeks and ourselves think of God, there are many great problems, which will be the matter of the next two chapters.

To be sure, superficial reflection supposes the opposite. It is commonly thought that trinitarian language about God marks Christianity's discontinuity with the Hebrew Scriptures. Increasingly, Hellenist Christians were supposedly led by their devotion to Jesus to divinize him and so to mitigate God's uniqueness. This common supposition is simply false. As we have seen, the triune shape of the Christian mission was immediately given by its claim to be Israel's eschatological mission, and the triune shape of the Thanksgiving by its fidelity to Jewish patterns of prayer. Further analyses of this kind could be made.

It is true—as we will see in the next chapter—that from about 150 A.D. Christianity's confrontation with Hellenism led to formulations which initially smacked of divinization. But—as we will also see—the whole developed doctrine of the Trinity was the church's effort to *resist* this temptation. And at that level of immediate trinitarian witness and experience which we are now discussing, and during the period before massive confrontation with Hellenic theology, there was not even incipient conflict between trinitarian and Hebrew interpretations of God. On the contrary, this immediate trinitarianism was, we assert, the only possible *fulfillment* of the Hebrew Scriptures.

Israel's interpretation of God was undoubtedly the historical result of a multitude of factors, many now untraceable. But systematically and at least in part historically, Israel's theology can all be derived from the identification of God by the Exodus. If God is, more than trivially, *the one who* rescued Israel from Egypt, the main characteristics of this God are immediately evident.[29]

First, Yahweh is not on the side of established order. The usual God, whose eternity is the Persistence of the beginning, has as his very honor among us that in him we are secure against the threats of the future. Ancient imperial peoples poignantly experienced the fragility of their achievement; the situation in which seed-time and harvest return each year had barely been secured, and the barbarian destroyer was each year at the door. The gods of the ancient civilizations simply *were* the Certainty of Return, the Guarantee of Continuance. Marduk, for example, was *the one who* back at the Beginning divided the Mesopotamian swamps into irrigated land and channeled water, and in that he was always still there the people could transcend the ever-renewed threat of relapse into pre-creation disorder. The damnation against which Yahweh fought for Israel was the precise opposite.

Israel understood itself not by an established order but by rescue from oppression under the archetypically standing order, that of Egypt. Throughout Israel's history, she longed to become an established state "like all the nations" (1 Sam. 8:4–5). But God always saw to it that Israel would fail, and the prophets regularly denounced the very attempt (1 Sam. 8:7–9). Indeed, and most uncanny of all, Yahweh remained free himself to undo the standing order of his own people; for example, "For, behold, [Yahweh, Yahweh] of hosts, is taking away from Jerusalem and from Judah stay and staff, the whole stay of bread, and the whole stay of water; the mighty man and the soldier, the judge and the prophet, the diviner and the elder" (Isa. 3:1–2).

Second, Yahweh's will is not identical with natural necessity—that is, his will is indeed what we mean by "will." In the great ancient myths, the beginning of the god's worship by his people is in each case identical with the absolute Beginning of all things. Just therein lay assurance: nothing can overthrow the people's Basis, since outside it there is nothing. Israel, on the other hand, knew very well of a history, including a history of Israel's own forefathers, that preceded the Exodus. The great myths of other peoples tell of a primeval event which set the pattern of time and is therefore above time, which never really ceases to happen—as Marduk's primeval separation of water and land recurred at each yearly inundation and draining. Israel's story told of an event which, for all repeated cultic celebration, had happened only once, *in* time rather than above time.

Israel, of course, could and did attribute general creation to its God. But Yahweh's creation of the world and his creation of Israel were two acts, not one. Israel knew that created reality did not necessarily include her, that Israel might not have been. Since Israel did nevertheless exist, by act of Yahweh, that act was just so understood as a *choice*:[30] "You have seen what I did to the Egyptians, and how I . . . brought you to myself. Now therefore . . . , you shall be my own possession among all peoples" (Exod. 19:4–5).

Third, since there was history before there was Israel, and yet the God of Israel ruled that history, the question is necessarily posed, How was Yahweh the God of Israel before there was Israel? The developed form of Israel's tradition had an answer: between Creation-times and the Exodus was the time of the fathers, of Abraham, Isaac, and Jacob. But how were these Israel? The solution of the ancient narrators was that patriarchal Israel was Israel by the *promise* of a land and a land's possibility of nationhood.[31] Abraham and the other fathers had lived in response to the promise that their descendants would be a great people. Having as yet no established order at all, the fathers had lived by the word that promised one.

Thus Israel knew itself as created by God's *word*, in the exact sense in which we until recently spoke of "a gentleman's word." Yahweh made a promise and kept it, and just so Israel came to be. From the start, salvation for Israel is given by promise of what is not yet, of the future that is now real only in the word that opens it. What other nations could say of a visible and tangible presence of God in holy images and places, Israel could say only of God's *utterance*: "The grass withers, the flower fades, but the word of our God will stand for ever" (Isa. 40:7–8). Moreover, Israel knew of a time when Israel had been

Israel *only* by this word, without security, when her whole existence had been hope. There remains only to note that with the Exile of 587 B.C., when all secure national existence was (at least until 1948 A.D.) taken away, historical Israel was put in exactly the position posited for the fathers.[32]

Yahweh's refusal of images (Exod. 20:4–6; Deut. 4:15–24; 5:8–9; 27:15) must be noted for its own sake, for the characteristics of Yahweh which we have just made into concepts were in Israel itself secured above all by this negative cultic rubric. No doubt there was a causal chain that led to this radical break with all ancient religion, but Israel's tradition did not preserve it. For Israel as for us, the prohibition of any image appeared as a sheer fact of revealed divine will, a main given of Yahweh's reality, one of the Ten Commandments (Exod. 20:1–17; Deut. 5:6–21. See Exod. 34:28; Deut. 4:13; 10:4).

This second commandment follows hard on the first. Indeed, the deuteronomistic theologians who shaped the present text regarded the second as the first's interpretation:[33] any god of whom an image can be made is merely thereby shown to be another god than Israel's. As to why this is so, the immediately next commandment gives the clue.[34] God has revealed his name, and the temptation to misuse this revelation must be resisted. But whereas God's name may be misused, his image is always misused. For with the name we *address* God, and just so give ourselves over to his freedom. The statue or picture, on the other hand, is our object, which we put where we choose; and if the promises of God are guaranteed by the presence of this object, then the past revelation that gave us the object puts the promised future in our control. Just this attempt at control is the confusion of Yahweh with other gods. It is the very confusion Israel in fact fell into with that other, initially unavoidable, objectification of God's presence, the temple, so that the prophets had always to combat those who appealed to "the temple of Yahweh" (Jer. 7:1–15), supposing that because God had once committed himself to the mount of Zion the future was secure for those who gathered on it.

Thus the identity of Israel's God, his difference from other gods, is precisely that he is not eternal in the way they are, that he is not God in the same way. That the past guarantees the future is exactly the deity of the gods, but Yahweh always challenges the past and everything guaranteed by it, from a future that is freedom. That is, the key steps of the trinitarian logic are the very specificity of the Hebrew Scriptures' interpretation of God. This comes to drastic expression in one strain of prophetic proclamation which appears above all in Ezekiel and Second Isaiah, the great prophets of the Exile.[35]

In this ripe and self-conscious strain of prophetic proclamation, all history is understood as a judgment in which it is the identity of God that is at stake. That the sequences of time embody the significance of *some* deity is taken as tautologous; the matter to be settled by the actual content of the sequences is *which* deity. And this decision is still future. Yahweh promises, by the word of his prophets, what he will do; and if it happens, all will know that the hidden meaning of events is his will, that "I am [Yahweh]" is true revelation. "Kings shall be your foster fathers, and their queens your nursing mothers. . . . Then you will know that I am [Yahweh]" (Isa. 49:23).

This futurity of God's final self-identification is not merely accidental, as if the exilic prophets just happened to write at a time when it had not yet occurred. God's identity was made problematic in Israel by a series of catastrophes which compelled the people to ask whether Yahweh were in fact the real Lord of events. And in the Exile itself, the very self-identity of Yahweh was made problematic, in a way which could be resolved only by a future event of the kind we call eschatological. The prophets asserted Yahweh's deity in the face of catastrophe by making also catastrophe his act, his act of judgment upon a faithless people: "You only have I known of all the families of the earth; therefore I will punish you for all your iniquities" (Amos 3:2). Since Yahweh nevertheless remained Israel's God, the prophets also proclaimed new liberating acts of Yahweh, new versions of all Israel's blessings, on the other side of catastrophe: "I will restore the fortunes of my people Israel. . . . I will plant them upon their land, and they shall never again be plucked up" (Amos 9:14–15). But what when the catastrophe is final? Is death? For that is the limit to which the Exile and the exilic prophets pushed God's judgment: "Thus says [Yahweh] to the land of Israel: An end! The end has come upon the four corners of the land. Now the end is upon you, and I will let loose my anger upon you" (Ezek. 7:2–3). Then the only possible new beginning is beyond the end, is the conquest of death, is resurrection. Then the only question, with which the Hebrew Scriptures in a real sense conclude, is: "Son of man, can these bones live?" (Ezek. 37:3). And since it is Yahweh who both judges and blesses, his own self-identity depends upon the answer. Only the resurrection of the dead will verify Yahweh's self-introduction as God, and when that event occurs the trinitarian logic promptly becomes explicit experience.

As to how, positively, Yahweh is eternal, Israel's interpretation is that he is faithful. Where other ancient religions said that God is beyond time, Israel said: "For ever, [Yahweh], thy word is firmly fixed in the heavens. Thy faithfulness endures to all generations; thou hast established the earth, and it stands fast" (Ps. 119:89–90). *Emunah* (faithfulness) is the reliability of a promise; thus the Revised Standard Version often translates it as "truth" (e.g., Prov. 12:17; Hos. 5:9), and a promise which is verified by events is "made *emun*" (e.g., 1 Kings 8:26). If God continues to bless Israel in spite of everything, it is because he "is keeping the oath which he swore" to the fathers, it is because "[Yahweh] is the *faithful* God who keeps covenant" (Deut. 7:8–9). And when the Fulfillment comes, when "kings shall see and arise," it will be "because of [Yahweh], who is faithful" (Isa. 49:7).

In one famous passage, the interpretation of God's eternity as faithfulness approaches a metaphysical definition. Within the tradition of the covenant with David, the most beautiful statement of Israel's hope proclaims: "I will make with you an everlasting covenant, my steadfast, sure love for David" (Isa. 55:3).

Unlike the normal gods, Yahweh does not transcend time

by immunity to it. The continuity of his being is not that of a defined entity, some of whose defining characteristics persist from beginning to end. It is rather the sort of continuity we have come to call "personal"; it is established in his words and commitments, by the faithfulness of his later acts to the promises made in his earlier acts. The continuity of his being transcends time, to be *eternal*, in that he keeps all his promises, in that time cannot take any of his commitments from him. It is just this interpretation of God's eternity that we introduced as the logical necessity—given the resurrection—of trinitarian identification of God.

Primary Trinitarianism

Therefore, so long as Christian interpretation of God was in unshaken continuity with that of the Hebrew Scriptures, Christian discourse and reflection shaped themselves naturally and unproblematically to the triune rhetorical space. This can be seen in the New Testament and so long thereafter[36] as the communities were not strongly confronted with Hellenic interpretation of God.

That "God" and God's "Spirit" form a rhetorical and conceptual pair for proclamation of God's work and interpretation of our life is entirely unproblematic in the New Testament. The use was imposed by the experience of Pentecost and needed no conceptual or linguistic innovation over against the Hebrew Scriptures. Also that "Christ" and the "Spirit" form such a pair in that the Spirit is *Christ's* Spirit was direct and—if the gospel is true—legitimate interpretation of the Hebrew Scriptures, asserting merely the fulfillment of certain expectations in fact contained therein and involving no conceptual or linguistic innovation (e.g., Isa. 11:1–9; 42:1).

That "God the Father" and "Jesus Christ his Son" form a similar pair is more complicated. It was of course the immediate consequence of that identification of God by Jesus' resurrection which is the whole import of the New Testament. But while the identification of God by historical events is fundamental in the Hebrew Scriptures, that the conclusively identifying events turn out to be the life of an individual person requires language beyond that of the Hebrew Scriptures, though in the New Testament itself never incongruous therewith. We cannot avoid a quick survey of these developments.[37]

The emergence of a semantic pattern in which the uses of "God" and "Jesus Christ" are mutually determining is fundamental. That pattern is firmly established before the earliest Pauline writings,[38] for example, the formula quoted by Paul, "If you confess with your lips that Jesus is Lord and believe in your heart that God raised him from the dead, you will be saved" (Rom. 10:9. See, e.g., Gal. 1:1; 2 Cor. 4:14). In Paul the standard Hebrew theological predicates take either God or Jesus as subject, or both at once:[39] for example, "grace" is interchangeably "of God" (Rom. 5:15) or "of Christ" (Rom. 16:20) or bestowed "from God our Father and the Lord Jesus Christ" (Rom. 1:7). Parallel constructions have "God" in one part and "Christ" in the other:[40] "So we are ambassadors for Christ, God making his appeal through us" (2 Cor. 5:20). For Paul, *God* will rule his kingdom, Jesus is *Lord*, and these two circumstances are one fact only: "For the kingdom of God [means] righteousness and peace . . . ; he who thus serves Christ is acceptable" (Rom. 14:17–18, e.g.). Christ simply *is* "the power of God and the wisdom of God" (1 Cor. 1:24), the manifestation of that "righteousness" in which Judaism summed up the godliness of God (Rom. 3:21–22). Yet "God" and "Christ" are not simply identified; thus prayer and thanksgiving are always directed *to* God, *through* Christ or "in his name."[41]

It is this semantic pattern which best displays the relation between the Father and Jesus, "the Son," as the apostolic church experienced it. The titles and images by which various groups more directly attempted to grasp the relation are for our present concern of secondary importance. We need only note primal Christianity's eclecticism in the drafting of such conceptions, and their general concord with the Hebrew Scriptures. Such mythic christology as appears, for example, in Philippians 2,[42] or the Book of Hebrews or John's Gospel, where Christ is a "pre-" or "postexistent" heavenly being of unstipulated relation to God displays a kind of thinking fully shared by contemporary Judaism[43] and well grounded in the Hebrew Scriptures.[44] The various christological titles by which the risen Lord was addressed and proclaimed are without exception functional in their import. They do not say what sort of "being" Christ has, but merely what role he has. Most typical in its logic is "Lord."[45] Initially merely Jesus' disciples' term of address to their master, it was naturally resumed for their risen Lord after the resurrection. But now this Lord is enthroned in God's own power and directs their mission by a Spirit that is God's own. In these circumstances, the Hebrew Scriptures' use of "Lord" for God himself cannot help but resonate with the in-itself still purely human title for Jesus. With the experience of the ancient church in our inheritance, *we* cannot but ask *what sort of being*—"divine," "human," or what—this title and the others used by the primal church attribute to Jesus. It is vital to understand that they raised no such question for the primal church itself, that the analysis, for example, just given of "Lord" completely describes what it did or could do for the apostolic users, and that this restriction does not describe a lack.

The resurrection compelled the apostolic church to find new language; only for us does this language raise questions over against the Hebrew Scriptures. The language once available, and given the logic of the Hebrew Scriptures' talk of God, Christian invocation, exhortation, and explanation seem to have taken triune form merely by following the path of least difficulty and quite without need for explicit reflection on the pattern itself. We will best assure ourselves of this by samples cited at near random from different strands of the New Testament: "But you, beloved . . . , pray in the Holy Spirit; keep yourselves in the love of God; wait for the mercy of our Lord Jesus Christ" (Jude 20–21; see 1 Pet. 1:2); "But it is God who establishes us with you in Christ . . . ; he has . . . given us his Spirit in our hearts as a guarantee" (2 Cor. 1:21–22);[46] "For through him [Christ] we both have access in one Spirit to the Father" (Eph. 2:18).[47] Nor is this merely a matter of stock phrases; the essential temporal logic appears in triune formulas lacking one or another of the standard titles, for example, "I charge you in the presence of *God*, and of *Christ Jesus* who is to judge the living and the dead, and by *his appearing and his kingdom*" (2 Tim. 4:1).[48] Again, "May the *God of hope* fill you with all joy and peace in *believing*, so that by the power of the *Holy Spirit* . . ."(Rom. 15:13).

The initial place in life of such language is doubtless displayed by the writer of Ephesians at 5:18–20: "But be filled with the Spirit, addressing one another in psalms and hymns and spiritual songs, singing and making melody to the Lord . . . giving thanks in the name of our Lord Jesus Christ to God the Father." The essential Christian experience was of assemblies gripped by the dynamism of a particular future—"his appearing and his kingdom"—which dynamism the Scriptures taught them to call "the Spirit" and in which grip all prayer and praise was to "God the Father" and in the name of the one under whose lordship we are indeed God's children and share his Spirit. Given this sort of liturgical experience, it is utterly natural for the work of salvation to be compendiously described simply by reversing the order and going through the same sequence starting with the Father, as does the same writer to the Ephesians: "In him, according to the purpose of him who accomplishes all things . . . , we who first hoped in Christ have been destined . . . to live for the praise of his glory. In him you also, who . . . have believed in him, were sealed with the promised Holy Spirit, which is the guarantee of our inheritance" (Eph. 1:11–14). Just so this writer obtains a complete framework for theology and can describe the entire Christian reality in the coordinates of "God's grace," "the mystery of Christ," and revelation "by the Spirit" (e.g., Eph. 3:2–6).

In this matter as in so many others, Paul's discourse is both the richest and the most precise. He can describe his own calling thus: "to be a minister of Christ Jesus . . . in the priestly service of the gospel of God, so that the offering of the Gentiles may be acceptable, sanctified by the Holy Spirit" (Rom. 15:16). Note the precision of the uses: Paul serves both "Jesus" and

"God," but his service of "God" is "priestly," whereas his service of Christ is discipleship, and the fruit of his service, offered to God, is made acceptable by the Spirit. In the proem to his Roman letter, he carefully distinguishes that the gospel is "of" God and "concerning" "his Son," then he locates the "power" of the Father-Son relation thus posited in "the Spirit of holiness" (Rom. 1:1–4). When Paul's special teaching of "justification" is to be fully and theologically described, we read: "Therefore, since we are justified by faith, we have peace *with* God *through* our Lord Jesus Christ [and this] hope does not disappoint us, because God's [note the genitive] love *has been poured into* our hearts *through* the Holy Spirit" (Rom. 5:1–5).

The most remarkable trinitarian passage in the New Testament, one amounting to an entire theological system, is the eighth chapter of Paul's letter to Rome. Its conceptual and argumentative heart is verse 11: "If the Spirit of him who raised Jesus from the dead dwells in you, he who raised Christ Jesus from the dead will give life to your mortal bodies also through his Spirit which dwells in you." The subject phrase displays in the uttermost conceptual compression the precise structure we have called "the trinitarian logic": the *Spirit* is "*of* him *who* raised *Jesus*." And from the prepositional structure of this phrase, Paul then develops a rhetoric and argument which sweeps justification and the work of Christ and prayer and eschatology and ethics and predestination into one coherent understanding.[49] With somewhat less dialectical and rhetorical complexity than in Romans 8, many other passages display what can only be called a standard Pauline trinitarian conceptuality. "God" is named as the agent of salvation, which is accomplished in an act described by such phrases as "in Christ Jesus," the purpose of which act, both eschatologically and penultimately, is a "sending" of the Spirit with "gifts" (e.g., 1 Cor. 1:4–8).

The new thing that appears in the immediate postapostolic church is the attempt not merely to speak in a trinitarian fashion, but to speak *about* the Trinity in explicit respect of his triuneness. This is done mostly by mythic metaphor. What we here have to examine is the trinitarianism of what Cardinal Daniélou somewhat misleadingly called "Jewish Christianity,"[50] that is, all Christianity up to the direct challenge of Hellenic thought around 150 A.D., and thereafter the Christianity of those areas not heavily so challenged. The principle of all this trinitarianism is classically stated by the epexegetical continuation of the saying of Clement earlier cited: "as of God, *as of the judge* of the living and the dead."[51] The equation of Christ— and the Spirit—with God is in all this thinking an attribution of function inseparable from God.

There were in the still-"Jewish" church a whole succession of function-images for the relation of Christ to God, the Spirit's relation to both not so often being problematical.[52] There was evidently a "name" christology: "The name of the Son of God is great and infinite and bears up the whole cosmos." There was a "Torah" christology. In contemporary Jewish wisdom-speculation, the Torah is the hypostasis, the tangible presence, of God's wisdom in Israel; just so for "Jewish" Christianity is the preached Christ in all nations. In Hermas' vision a great tree appears and is interpreted: "This great tree, which over-shadows . . . the whole earth, is God's law that is given to all the world. And that law is the Son of God, as he is proclaimed to the ends of the earth." Again, Christ was called the "Cov-enant," the embracing bond between God and his people; the "Scepter" by which God rules us; the "Beginning" of Genesis 1:1; even the "Day" of Genesis 1.[53]

In Ignatius there appears a "Logos" christology very differ-ent from the later speculation we will have to consider. Here "the Word" means God's utterance, by which he breaks his silence: "There is one God, who has manifested himself by Jesus Christ his Son, who is his word proceeding from silence, who obeyed the one who sent him."[54] In the otherness of the utterance over against the speaker, Christ is then "the knowl-edge of God," "the mouth" of God, "the intention of God"[55] and just so he can also be called simply "God."[56] What would have come of *this* Logos mythology we can only guess.

A "Spirit" christology was an obvious and inevitable development,[57] since in the Hebrew Scriptures the "Spirit" was already established as somehow a pair to "God." Such a christology appears in the earliest strata of tradition preserved in the New Testament (e.g., Rom. 1:2). More blunt than Clement one could not be: "Christ . . . was first Spirit and became flesh."[58] But even so, Christ and the Spirit could not simply be equated, since Christ *gives* the Spirit. Thus on this line we get a true Trinity-image very quickly: "The preexistent Holy Spirit, creator of all creatures, God made dwell in flesh which he chose. And this flesh . . . served the Spirit well, walking in holiness and chastity. . . . Therefore [God] assumed [this flesh] as a fellow of the Holy Spirit. . . . He took this son to be his counselor . . . , so that also this flesh . . . might have his dwelling place."[59] Here the Son, but not the Spirit, becomes God by adoption. This was a frequent notion.[60]

Probably the most important of the "Jewish" Trinity-images evoked the Son and the Spirit as "angels." In the most ancient postapostolic church there was undoubtedly an angel christology, immediately dependent on apocalyptic Judaism's angel speculation.[61] But there was an angel pneumatology too, on the same basis.[62] And so the full trinitarian experience of God found expression, as in the apocalyptic vision of Isaiah: "And I saw him [Christ] ascend into the seventh heaven, and all the saints and angels praised him. And I saw him sit down on the right hand of the Glory. . . . And the Angel of the Holy Spirit I saw sitting on the left hand."[63] This vision of God and his two great angels seems to have had great continuing importance for the later development of trinitarianism; Origen, creator of the first great trinitarian theology, repeatedly prooftexts with Isaiah 6:1–3, interpreting the two seraphim of that passage as allegories of the Son and the Spirit and explicitly attributing this interpretation to a Jewish teacher.[64]

We now find this angel christology and angel trinitarianism alarming—as indeed the other "Jewish" Trinity images. It seems to create a large class of demigods and locate Christ and the Spirit among them, surely a case of "divinization," and

halfhearted at that. But this happens only because we anach-
ronistically project our question about *kinds* of being back on
this essentially Semitic discourse, and are then disappointed[65]
to find Christ and the Spirit not fully divine, and Christ not
fully human either. In this thinking itself, an angel is simply
one to whom God gives a mission and whose own reality is
constituted by this mission. Nothing is thereby suggested
about what sort of being is possessed by either God or this
manifestation.[66] It can well be that the mission is in fact God's
own mission. If it is, this will simply appear in descriptions of
what the angel does—he judges all men, forgives sin, or whatever.[67] And that Christ and the Spirit are transcendent over
"other" angels appears iconographically, as in Hermas, where
Christ is bigger than the other archangels and is a seventh,
when all know the full number of archangels is six, or as in the
Ascension of Isaiah where God and the two great angels are
together worshiped by the other angels.[68]

The kinds of trinitarian discourse developed in the New Testament and in the immediately subsequent period have continued through the history of the church. With use of the triune
name they are the substance of living trinitarian apprehension
of God. Christians bespeak God in a triune coordinate system;
they speak *to* the Father, *with* the Son, *in* the Spirit, and only
so bespeak *God*. Indeed, they live in a sort of temporal space
defined by these coordinates, and just and only so live "in
God." And they represent the God with whom they have thus
to do, in iconography and metaphor which is functional in its
attribution of deity. Where these modes lose some of their
power to shape actual proclamation and prayer, as in the medieval and the modern Western church, an alienation of the
church must be suspected.

Pastors often suppose the Trinity to be too complicated to
explain to the laity. Nothing could be more misguided. Believers *know how* to pray to the Father, daring to call him "Father"
because they pray with Jesus his Son, and so enter into the
future these two have for them, that is, praying in the Spirit.
Those who know how to do this, and who realize that just in

the space defined by these coordinates they have to do with God, do understand the Trinity. All the intellectual complexities we must shortly embark upon are a secondary phenomenon, whose proper location is the back of the teacher's and preacher's mind, determining the way he guides and, when necessary, explains, this relation to this God.

The Three-Article Creeds

The structures of language and experience analyzed in the previous two sections are not merely in fact present in the life of the church. They are daily and explicitly acknowledged and proclaimed as fundamental by the worshiping assemblies of all Christendom, being embodied in the great liturgical creeds of the apostles and of Nicaea. The three-article creeds are the daily education and public self-definition of the Christian community in all its branches, recited at baptism and often at the Supper or other main services. And they are acknowledged such by Eastern, Roman Catholic, and Reformation bodies alike—as, for example, in the Lutheran *Book of Concord,* where they are put in the first place and aptly called the ecumenical creeds.

Creedal formulations are as old as the gospel. The proclamation of the gospel, and the interior verbal life of the gospel's community, had specific content from the very beginning, for they involved cultivating the religious tradition of a particular people, also among persons not raised in it; telling a particular narrative, of what happened with Jesus; and making a particular promise, of what could be expected because this Jesus lives. Under the universal conditions of the life of any continuing community, standard patterns and formulas of proclamatory and liturgical statement of faith necessarily appeared.[69] They were needed in a variety of situations and therefore took a variety of forms. For our immediate purposes two forms are important.

First, the initial preachers and catechists and their successors used and passed on narrative summaries of the chief claims and facts about Jesus. We are not dependent on mere conjecture here. Paul tells us explicitly that "the gospel" which he preached to the Corinthians was "handed on" to and by him. He then rehearses the items: "that Christ died for our sins in accordance with the scriptures, that he was buried, that he was raised on the third day in accordance with the scriptures, and that he appeared to Cephas, then to the twelve. . . ." (1 Cor. 15:1–7). There are numerous other such summaries cited or alluded to in the New Testament.[70] Of these, some have a feature we must note: they are attached to confession of faith in God and so come out, quite unselfconsciously, trinitarian, simply setting faith in God and faith in "Christ Jesus" alongside each other (Rom. 1:3–4; 9:34; 2 Tim. 2:8; 1 Pet. 3:18ff.).[71]

Second, there is the rubric that baptism is to be "in the name of the Father and of the Son and of the Holy Spirit." We do not know what liturgical form this naming initially took, or even if it took the same form in all communities,[72] but by the time ancient baptismal practice emerges into clear view,[73] in the writings of Hippolytus at the turn of the second and third centuries, the naming is an interrogation of trinitarian confession: "Let the baptizer . . . say, 'Do you believe in God the Father Almighty? Do you believe in Christ Jesus, the Son of God . . . ? Do you believe in the holy, good, and life-giving Spirit?' "[74] There are signs that such interrogation may have been the—or an—original way of baptismal "naming"; in any case, the primal church did demand the confession of faith at baptism,[75] and this confession was shaped by the triune pattern of baptismal naming, however the latter was done.

The sort of declaratory creeds we know and use, such as the Apostles' Creed or the creeds used as bases by the councils of Nicaea and Constantinople, developed from the fusion of these two forms: the baptismal questions with their canonically stipulated triune pattern, and the summaries of christological narrative.[76] It seems likely that the location of this development was catechetical discipline which had both to prepare for baptism and to reinforce the main items of christological missionary preaching. The shift to declaratory from interrogatory

form—which was retained at baptism itself—was probably oc-
casioned by the demand that the catechumen, before baptism,
report to the congregation his participation in the faith into
which the congregation had been baptized: "I believe—as do
you—in. . . ." It also seems likely that the earliest stable product of this development was the forerunner of the Apostles'
Creed, the old creed of the church of Rome, fixed sometime
toward the end of the second century. This Roman creed was
created by addition of the christological kerygma "who was
conceived by" to a trinitarian baptismal interrogation about
"God the Father Almighty, and . . . Christ Jesus, his only Son,
our Lord, and the Holy Spirit, the holy church, the resurrection
of the flesh."[77]

As Tertullian remarked, this form of baptismal interrogation
is already a "somewhat fuller" version of the naming Christ
commanded,[78] enriched with explanatory identifications of
"Father" and "Son," and with urgent items of baptismal faith
appended to "Holy Spirit."[79] The expansion may have been
the result of another previous conflation. There may have been
catechetical lists of theological rather than kerygmatic items, of
no special number, which the baptismal interrogation drew
into itself.[80] In this case we have yet another instance of the
trinitarian name's remarkable ability to impose its pattern on
Christian discourse. Or the expansion may simply be the result
of a natural explanatory impulse at baptism's decisive moment:
"Do you believe in the Father—who is the one almighty God?"
And so on.[81] Either way or both, the expansive impulse oper-
ated not only in Rome but in the Eastern communities as well,
and with similar results.[82]

The Apostles' Creed and creeds like it were created by the
catechetical and liturgical affinity, and the logical fit, between
the triune baptismal name of God and the evangelical history
narrated in the gospel. That is, it is exactly the logic analyzed
earlier in this chapter, which the creeds declare to be the true
and necessary logic of the gospel.

One feature of the standard creeds, especially the Apostles'
Creed, has regularly proven misleading: their first article's

identification of the Father simply with "God," while the Son and the Spirit are identified as "of" and "from" God. In this, of course, the creeds follow New Testament usage. The pattern seems to suggest that the Father is God by himself, that one would not need to consider the Son or the Spirit to be considering God—contrary to the logic we have just surveyed and to the insight gained in the controversies next to be considered, that only the Trinity as such is God by himself. This suggestion has indeed been taken as the basis for rejection of the whole trinitarian logic and doctrine, perhaps most notably by none less than Friedrich Schleiermacher.[83]

Such conclusions are superficial. The creeds are confessional and doxological utterances, and they follow precisely the prayer and praise structure of Scripture, where "God" is a term of address and where it is indeed *to* the Father that the address is made. But the decisive gospel-insight is that if we only pray *to* God, if our relation to God is reducible to the "to" and is not decisively determined also by "with" and "in," then it is not the true God whom we identify in our address, but rather some distant and timelessly uninvolved divinity whom we have envisaged. We pray indeed *to* the Father, and so usually address the Father simply as "God." But we address *this* Father in that and only in that we pray *with* Jesus *in* their Spirit. The particular God of Scripture does not just stand over against us; he envelops us. And only by the full structure of the envelopment do we have this God.

NOTES

1. Gregory of Nyssa *Against Eunomius*, in his *Opera*, vols. 1–2, ed. W. Jaeger (Leiden: Brill, 1960), 3/7.53.13.

2. Martin Luther, WA 18:597–787; 43:435–59. See Eberhard Jüngel, "Quae supra nos, nihil ad nos," *EvTH* 32 (1972): 197–240.

3. WA 18:619

4. Ibid., p. 633.

5. On the subsequent history of the mission, Ferdinand Hahn,

Das Verständnis der Mission im Neuen Testament (Neukirchen-Vluyn: Erziehungsverein, 1962).

6. See ibid., pp. 32–33.

7. Ibid.

8. Ibid., pp. 37ff.

9. Whether the postresurrection command imitates the precrucifixion sending or is read back into it is unimportant here.

10. On this and the following, see ibid., pp. 13–14.

11. Ibid., pp. 37–74.

12. The enthronement of the Risen One was at the heart of the faith very early. Phil. 2:9–11, a pre-Pauline hymn, must date from almost immediately after the resurrection.

13. Ibid., pp. 52ff.

14. This is the stereotypical pattern of the story told in Acts.

15. See Robert W. Jenson, *Visible Words* (Philadelphia: Fortress Press, 1978), pp. 67–74, with bibliography.

16. Louis Bouyer, *Eucharist*, trans. G. Quinn (Notre Dame: University of Notre Dame Press, 1968), pp. 91–226, 309–10.

17. Jenson, *Visible Words*, pp. 68ff., with bibliography.

18. Ibid., pp. 71ff., with bibliography.

19. *Prex Eucharistica*, ed. M. Haenggi and I. Pahl (Freiburg i. B., 1961), p. 128.

20. J. Armitage Robinson, in the introduction to his edition of *Irenaeus: The Demonstration of the Apostolic Teaching* (London: SPCK, 1920), pp. 30–40.

21. Georg Kretschmar, *Studien zur frühchristlichen Trinitätstheologie* (Tübingen: J. C. B. Mohr, 1956), pp. 182–96.

22. D. Jenkins, ed., "Origen: Commentary on I Corinthians," *JThS* 9 (1908): 502.

23. Jenson, *Visible Words*, pp. 95–104.

24. I ignore various Protestant orders made up only of bits and pieces from the disintegrated Roman order; most have no rationale at all.

25. I assume the Antiochene order; the Alexandrian placement of the epiclesis between the Sanctus and the Narrative of Institution had no theological motivation.

26. See 2 *Clement* 1.1–2; the diction is already turning to face Hellenism; the Bible does not so much "think *about*" God as speak *for* him.

27. Thus Ignatius, who has the Greek diction, a Logos-concept, and

treats the ascription of deity and temporality to one subject as a paradox, nevertheless refers to Jesus simply as God, without noting a problem; *Letter to the Ephesians* 8.2; 19.2; *Letter to the Smyrneans* 1.1. And for Ignatius these expressions are equivalent to ascriptions of a functional relation of Christ to God; *Ephesians* 17.2; *Letter to the Romans* 8.2.

28. Thus "Clement" exegetes his own dictum in 2 *Clement* 1:1–2: ". . . as about the judge of the living and the dead."

29. Walther Zimmerli, *Old Testament Theology in Outline,* trans. D. E. Green (Atlanta: John Knox, 1978), pp. 21–32. For the opposite standard pattern, Mircea Eliade, *Cosmos and History* (New York: Harper & Row, 1959).

30. Zimmerli, *Theology,* pp. 43ff.

31. Ibid., pp. 27–32.

32. E.g., Walther Zimmerli, "Die Bedeutung der grossen Schriftprophetie für das altestamentliche Reden von Gott," *VT.S,* 1972, pp. 63–64.

33. Walther Zimmerli, "Das Zweite Gebot," in *Festschrift für Alfred Bertholet zum 80. Geburtstag,* ed. Walter Baumgartner et al. (Tübingen: J. C. B. Mohr, 1960), pp. 550–57.

34. Ibid., pp. 558ff.

35. To the following paragraph, see the classic study of Walther Zimmerli, *Erkenntnis Gottes nach dem Buche Ezekiel,* AthANT 27 (Zurich: Zwingli-Verlag, 1954). I will not provide my own apparatus, since it would only reproduce his.

36. I.e., in what Jean Daniélou, *The Theology of Jewish Christianity,* trans. J. Baker (London: Darton, Longman & Todd, 1964), somewhat misleadingly calls "Jewish Christianity."

37. For a start on the immense amount of literature, G. Sevenster, "Christologie des Urchristentums," *RGG*[3] 1:1745–62.

38. Klaus Wengst, *Christologische Formeln und Lieder des Urchristentums,* StNT 7 (Gütersloh: Gütersloher Verlagshaus, 1972).

39. See now Wolfgang Schrage, "Theologie und Christologie bei Paulus und Jesus," *EvTh* 36 (1976): 123–35.

40. Ibid., p. 125.

41. Ibid., pp. 127–28.

42. On the exegesis of this passage, see the discussion of it in Ernst Lohmeyer, *Die Briefe an die Philipper, an die Kolosser und an Philemon,* 11th ed., KEK 9 (Göttingen: Vandenhoeck & Ruprecht, 1956).

43. Wilhelm Bousset, *Die Religion des Judentums,* ed. H. Gressmann, 3d ed. (Tübingen: J. C. B. Mohr, 1966), pp. 302–57.

44. From the "angel of the Lord" in the patriarchal narratives (e.g., Gen. 23:9–19) to the great eschatological figure of Dan. 7:13–14.

45. E.g., Ferdinand Hahn, *Christologische Hoheitstitel* (Göttingen: Vandenhoeck & Ruprecht, 1964), pp. 67–132.

46. Elsewhere in Paul: Rom. 14:17–18; 15:30; 1 Cor. 2:2–5; 12:4–6; 2 Cor. 3:3; Phil. 3:3; 1 Thess. 5:18–20.

47. Elsewhere in this literature: Eph. 1:11–14; 1:17; 2:18–22; 3:2–7; 3:14–17; 4:4–6; 5:18–20; Col. 1:6–8; Titus 3:4–6.

48. It is regularly "Spirit" that is omitted as word but present in substance; e.g., 1 Pet. 1:3.

49. See Peter von der Osten-Sacken, *Römer 8 als Beispiel paulinischer Theologie* (Göttingen: Vandenhoeck & Ruprecht, 1975).

50. Daniélou, *Theology*.

51. *2 Clement* 1.2.

52. On the following, Daniélou, *Theology*, pp. 147–66; Aloys Grillmeier, *Christ in Christian Tradition*, trans. J. S. Bowden (New York: Sheed & Ward, 1965), 1:41–53.

53. Hermas *Similitudes* 9.14.5; 8.3.2.

54. Ignatius *Letter to the Magnesians* 8.2.

55. Ignatius *Ephesians* 17.2; 3.2; *Romans* 8.2.

56. Ignatius *Ephesians* 7.2; 18.2; *Smyrneans* 1.

57. Jaroslav Pelikan, *The Christian Tradition: A History of the Development of Doctrine*, vol. 1, *The Emergence of the Catholic Tradition (100–600)* (Chicago: University of Chicago Press, 1971), pp. 184ff.

58. *2 Clement* 9.5.

59. Hermas *Similitudes* 5.6.5–6. In yet another strain, the Spirit was evidently seen as Jesus' Mother, also giving a Trinity image; Georg Kretschmar, *Studien zur frühchristlichen Trinitätstheologie* (Tübingen: J. C. B. Mohr, 1956), pp. 20–22.

60. See Pelikan, *Emergence*, pp. 176ff.

61. Daniélou, *Theology*, pp. 117–47; Johannes Barbel, *Christos Angelos* (Bonn: Hanstein, 1941), pp. 181–311; Martin Werner, *The Formation of Christian Doctrine* (New York: Harper & Row, 1957), pp. 120–81; Aloys Grillmeier, *Christ in Christian Tradition*, (New York: Sheed & Ward, 1965), pp. 46ff.

62. Daniélou, *Theology*, pp. 128ff.

63. *Ascension of Isaiah* 11.32–35. For other manifestations, Kretschmar, *Studien*, pp. 71–124.

64. E.g., Origen *Commentary on Isaiah* 1.2; 1.4; 41; *Commentary on*

Ezekiel 14.2; *On First Principles* 1.3.4; 4.3.14. See also Kretschmar, *Studien,* pp. 220–23.

65. Or we may be gleeful if we oppose the later doctrines of true Godhead and believe ourselves now to discover that the earliest church contradicted them. This is Martin Werner's rather primitive blunder, which invalidates all the arguments of his energetic and otherwise admirable investigations.

66. Daniélou, *Theology,* pp. 117ff.

67. E.g., Hermas *Similitudes* 8.1–2.

68. Ibid., 9.12.7–8; *Ascension of Isaiah* 8.16–18.

69. The standard presentation is J. N. D. Kelly, *Early Christian Creeds* (London: Longmans, Green, 1950), pp. 6–29.

70. Ibid., pp. 17ff.

71. See ibid.

72. The familiar declaration "I baptize you in the name . . ." is (so far as we know) a much later development.

73. Cf. ibid., pp. 40–49.

74. Hippolytus *Apostolic Tradition* 21.

75. Kelly, *Creeds,* pp. 40ff.

76. Ibid., pp. 30–130.

77. Ibid., pp. 119ff.

78. Tertullian *On the Crown* 3.

79. Thus, at the turn of the second and third centuries there seem to have been baptismal interrogations with five questions concerning Father, Son, Spirit, church, baptism. The last three went with one washing. Kelly, *Creeds,* pp. 82ff.

80. Cf. Kretschmar, *Studien.*

81. Cf. Kelly, *Creeds,* pp. 131ff.

82. Ibid., pp. 167–204.

83. See Wilfried Brandt, *Der Heilige Geist und die Kirche bei Schleiermacher* (Zurich: Zwingli-Verlag, 1968), pp. 226–65.

3

"Of One Being with the Father"

The Hellenic Interpretation of God

In much of this chapter we have a story to tell. The gospel mission did in fact meet with another and fundamentally incompatible identification of God, that of the Greeks, which could not be ignored. Christianity as we know it, and especially our inherited body of developed trinitarian doctrine and analysis, is the result. Such discourse as "of one being with the Father" or "one substance in three persons" is not spun from a sheer internal conceptuality of the faith. Its meaning occurs in the confrontation of biblical proclamation with Hellenic religion and reflection, and its elucidation therefore requires narrative of this event.

If the gospel had not met an incompatible identification of God in the Greek interpretation of deity, it would have met one in some other—and indeed it did and does in those branches of the mission that lead to great culture areas other than that in which our narrative is set. It will be by reluctance to take time seriously for God that any normal interpretation of God will clash with the gospel, so that any possible great missionary theology must contain some functional equivalent of the developed trinitarian teaching we are about to describe. But we can pursue this no further here. The gospel's initial history in non-Hellenic worlds was terminated by Islam, and its new history in them is, theologically, just beginning.

Hellenic theology was from the beginning an exact antagonist of biblical faith.[1] Israel's interpretation of God was determined by the rescue of wandering tribes from oppression under an established civilization, Greece's by an established civilization's overthrow by just such tribes. The flourishing religious and material world of Mycenaean Greece was swept away by the flood of Dorian tribes from the north. But in certain areas the memory and traditions of lost glory survived. When Greek civilization began to revive in the ninth century, it was these Ionians that led the way. Thus the historical memory of Greece began with catastrophe, with a national experience of sheer irrational contingency and power, and of death and destruction brought by it. Greek religion and reflection were tragic from their root; they were a sustained attempt to deal with the experience "that we must call no one blessed until he sees his last day, without disaster."[2] Greek religion and reflection were thereby imprinted with five characters important for our purpose.

First their driving question was, as formulated by Aristotle, "Can it be that *all* things pass away?"[3] In the myth of Chronos, the primeval father who devoured all his children, the Greeks stated their experience of time and its surprises: what Time produces, Time destroys. Their religion was the determination that Time not be supreme, that he be overthrown by a true "Father of gods and men." Greek religion was the quest for a rock of ages, resistant to the flow of time, a place or part or aspect of reality immune to change. The gods' one defining character was therefore immortality, immunity to destruction. Yahweh was eternal by his faithfulness *through* time; the Greek gods' eternity was their abstraction *from* time. Yahweh's eternity is thus intrinsically a matter of relation to his creatures—supposing there are any—whereas the Greek gods' eternity is the negation of such relation.

Second, Greek religion and reflection were an act of human self-defense against mysterious power and inexplicable contingency, that is, against just what mankind has mostly called "God." Homer is not only our chief witness to this; his poems became the Bible of Greece. The Ionian survivors willed that history have a humanly comprehensible pattern, of such a kind that its events be in principle predictable and planable. If superhuman—that is, immortal—actors were needed to explain some events and so vindicate their sense, these too had to be understandable and predictable in their motivations and reasons. Such were the "Olympian" gods, the Ionians' rationalized versions of various inherited nature and clan deities, whose singular lack of holiness and mystery scholars have always noted. The Ionians rescued themselves from chaos by enlightenment, by explanation of time's seeming mysteries.

Homer's successors as religious thinkers were the Ionian philosophers.[4] With them the reduction of all godly characteristics to one, immortality, and the inclusion also of the gods within one comprehensible scheme of events led—and this is the third character on our list—to the concept of "the divine," a unitary abstraction of godly Explanatory Power in and behind the plural gods of daily religion: "the Unbounded has no beginning . . . , but seems rather to be the Beginning of all other realities, and to envelop and control them. . . . This is the Divine. So the opinion of Anaximander and most of the natural philosophers."[5] For the educated class of Greece's classic period, this abstraction, often called "Zeus," was the true religious object: Timelessness simply as such.

Fourth, the quest for timeless reality is never satisfied by anything directly presented in our experience. All the world we see, hear, and touch does indeed pass away. If there is the Divine, it must therefore be above or behind or beneath or within the experienced world. It must be the Bed of time's river, the Foundation of the world's otherwise unstable structure, the Track of heaven's hastening lights. Greek religion and reflection, by their inner function, were "metaphysical," a quest for the timeless Ground of temporal being, that just so is a different sort of being than we ever immediately encounter.

And fifth, Greek religion and reflection were precisely the quest we have been calling them, for since the timeless Ground is never directly presented in experience, it has to be searched for. A whole complex of motifs that will be centrally important for our story are involved here. Greek apprehension of God is accomplished by penetrating through the temporal experienced world to its atemporal Ground. This theology is there-

fore essentially negative. The true predicates of deity are negations of predicates that pertain to experienced reality by
virtue of its temporality. God is "invisible," "intangible," "impassible" (i.e., unaffected by external events), "indescribable."[6]
This theology is essentially analogical, for while it consists in
negations of predicates that apply to the temporal world, it
cannot dispense with such predicates. The pattern is always
"Deity is F, only not as other, temporal, reality is F." The
method of interpreting God by analogy between our temporal
perfections and his timeless attributes is not a theologically
neutral device. Its use is the posit of a particular God, the Deity
of Hellenic religion.[7] Next this theology raises the question of
true deity, of the characteristics marking the final and so *real*
Ground, for if deity must be searched for, we have to be able
to recognize it when we find it. And finally this theology's
penetration to true deity is accomplished by mind,[8] that is, not
by discursive analysis or argument but by instantaneous intellectual intuition, by a sort of interior mirroring, in the
"mind's eye," for what is to be grasped is a timeless pattern.

Thus the essential pattern of Greek interpretation of God, in
daily religion and in the philosophy to which it gave birth.
Before returning to the main line of our narrative, we must
note one great event in the history of this religion.

The posit of Timelessness was initially sustaining. Deity was
posited as the reliable meaning and foundation of the human
world, but only a sort of blink of the metaphysical eye was
needed for the value-signs to reverse themselves. Hellenic theology posited timeless and temporal reality as different kinds
of being, defined by mutual negation, and all meaning and
value were located in timeless being. If we blink, we may suddenly see the line between as a barrier, shutting us out from
meaning, for we are temporal. Without attempting to assign
causes, it is enough for our purpose to record that, in the transition from the local polities of classic Greece to cosmopolitan
"Hellenism," this reversal of values occurred.[9]

Thus the dominant religious apprehension of late antiquity,
of the world to which the gospel came, was of Deity's *distance*—

not of his hiding—created by the very characteristics that made it Deity. We are in time, and God is not, and just so our situation is desperate. Therefore the religion of late antiquity was a frenzied search for mediators, for beings of a third ontological kind *between* time and Timelessness, to bridge the gap.[10] Already Socrates had posited such a third kind, Eros, the child of Fullness and Want, and perceived that the language appropriate to speak of this realm is myth, that is, ultimately false stories about divine beings, speech about eternity *as if* it were time.[11] Discourse about deity was in any case understood to be analogical. The word "god" is basically adjectival and thus applicable in various grades to Deity itself and to any mediators one or more steps down. In cosmopolitan Hellenism, such doctrine was put into desperate practice. All the vast heritage of the world's savior-gods, demigods, reified abstractions, and mid-beings generally were pressed into mediatorial service as almost-gods. It was inevitable that when the gospel appeared on this scene, "Christ" would be too.

The Initial Christianizing of Hellenism

When the gospel mission confronts the Hellenic interpretation of God, it cannot and could not simply reject it, for if the God of Israel and unconditional assurance in his name are to be proclaimed to all men, the God of Israel must be in fact mighty for all men. When someone asks, "But is Israel's God really God? Can all reality be interpreted as grounded in this God of Israel?" the mission must respond affirmatively. Israel proclaimed Yahweh as God for all peoples; in confrontation with Hellenism, this had to mean the claim that Israel's is the *real* God posited by Hellas' philosophers.[12]

Moreover, Hellenism's interpretation of God both caused and expressed late antiquity's chief religious problem, the distance of God. Therefore it was to this experience of distance from the divine that the comfort of the gospel had to be brought. If the message of Jesus' resurrection is to be a promise to those who suffer this distance, it must be promise about the

God whose distance is felt. That Yahweh is near can be no comfort to those mourning Zeus' departure, unless, somehow, Yahweh is the one and only real God and so is what Zeus claimed to be.

The confrontation could only be performed from within Hellenism. Only those who shared Hellas' quest, and the anguish in which it had terminated, could interpret them by Jesus' resurrection. There has been much talk of the "hellenization of Christianity," but that is an obverse description of the event, more straightforwardly to be called the "christianizing of Hellenism." The pastors and teachers who first carried the meeting of "Deity" and Yahweh were not, after all, first Christians who had to discover how to be Hellenists, but first Hellenists who had to find how to be Christian.

The gospel's experience of Hellenism is as old as the gospel. The Judaism of which Christianity was a shoot was itself a much syncretized and multiform phenomenon. The New Testament already reveals complicated histories of adaptation and transformation of Hellenic language and myth, but it was at the middle of the second century that Christian thinkers first posed the Hellenic analytic tasks to themselves as explicit matter for reflection, and it is there that we begin our narrative.

However the confrontation might have begun, it was in fact begun thus: Both bodies of discourse about God, the biblical and the Hellenic, were simply set alongside each other and more or less well carpentered together, depending on skill. On the one side, this meant that Christians took over the procedure of penetrating to the "real" God by abstracting from time with negative analogies. Thus even Theophilus of Antioch, the most biblical of mid-century thinkers, assumes without question that God is to be discovered behind and from his "works . . . , just as the soul in a man is not seen . . . , but is intuited by the movement of the body"; this intuition was to be achieved by purification of an inner mirror.[13] Accordingly, Christians also adopted the negative predicates by which Hellenism had qualified true deity, and made one composite list with items from biblical language.[14]

Already Ignatius, in 125 A.D., adopted the central and least biblical concept of late Hellenic theology: God is "impassible," immune to being acted upon.[15] This concept was to be the clearest and most troubling mark of Hellenic interpretation within Christian theology.[16] Justin Martyr, the most influential second-century theologian, defined "God" as the eternally self-caused and changeless cause of the being of all others,[17] to the satisfaction of believers and unbelievers alike. For Justin and his fellows, God is therefore "unoriginated," "unutterable," "immovable," "impassible," "inexpressible," "invisible," "unchangeable," "unplaceable," "immaterial," "unnamable," and so on.[18]

Yet these same theologians could also speak of God in incisively and even creatively biblical fashion. So Justin again: God is concerned with us; he is the "just overseer" of our lives;[19] he is compassionate and patient (the flat contradiction of "impassible");[20] his omnipotence is exercised above all in Jesus' resurrection;[21] he actively intervenes to reward and punish;[22] his course of action is determined by regard for us;[23] and his providence is both for the world and for "you and me."[24] The true God, indeed, is to be identified as the one who led Israel from Egypt.[25] Such language is not mediated with the negative analogical theology; the two conceptions of God are not so much synthesized as merely added together.[26] It is this additive tactic which has from the Apologists to the present remained standard in theology.

What must be said of Christ to speak the gospel is in each case the opposite of some predicate of the negative theology; the central example is "suffered under Pontius Pilate" versus "impassible." Therefore, speaking of Christ "as of" *this* God is a neat trick. The first device was what we may call the paradox christology. It is already full-blown in Ignatius: "There is one healer: fleshly and spiritual; originated and unoriginated; God in the flesh; true life in death; both from Mary and from God, first passible and then impassible."[27] The human-temporal side of the paradox-rhetoric is built of both abstract descriptions of temporality—for example, "visible," "mortal"—

and narration of Jesus' life and passion.[28] The other side of the rhetoric is made of standard predicates of Hellenic theology.

Through history the paradox christology has been a sign that the biblical interpretation of God is still alive in the church,[29] that Hellenic religion has not utterly driven it out. The paradox christology is also the only actual content of the "two natures" christology to be dogmatized by the Council of Chalcedon. Indeed, the formulas of that christology already appear in the earliest paradox rhetoric.[30] But the paradox christology cannot itself provide a satisfactory apprehension of God, being merely a christological reflection of the problem—the unsynthesized duality of God's identification on the one hand by impassibility, and so on, and on the other hand by what happens with Jesus. Somehow the paradox must be overcome. Before Christians nerved themselves to that, they inevitably tried first if the paradox could not merely be softened enough to live with. This can be and was done either by softening the human side or by softening the deity side.

In each direction, moreover, the paradox can be softened in two ways: by fudging the predicate or fudging the copula. "The Impassible is passible" can be softened to "The Impassible is almost-passible" (Apollinaris!) or "The Impassible is closely but not entirely identified with the passible" (Nestorius!). These evasions are the christological "heresies" of "Eutychianism" and "Nestorianism" and lead outside this book. In the other direction, "The passible is Impassible" can be softened to "The passible is almost-Impassible" or to "The passible is almost identifiable with the Impassible." The first is traditionally labeled "subordinationism," the second "modalism." They are the thread of our story.

The immediate question of every Hellenist hearing the gospel's talk of God the Beginning and God who is our fellow man Jesus and God the Fulfillment must be: But what is the timelessly self-identical Something that *is* all these three? What is the time-immune Continuity which must be the Being of the real God? If we are not firm enough to challenge the question, there are only two possible answers: It is a fourth, of which the three are only temporal manifestations, or It is one of the three (which must then be the Father, since the other two are "from" him), of which the other two are only temporal manifestations. The first move is "modalism," the second "subordinationism." Together, they comprise the whole list of ancient trinitarian heresies. They are heresies because they speak of God in just the way that saws off our narrative limb, because they insist on so interpreting God "himself" that no history can be told of him, so that the specific Christian identification of God cannot "really" be true. They are precisely as common and contrary to the gospel now as in the second and third centuries. In history they had to be worked through to be found out.

Modalism is the teaching that God himself is above time and the distinctions of Father, Son, and Spirit but appears successively in these roles to create, redeem, and sanctify.[31] From modalism's first recorded appearance in Rome, around 190 A.D., it was the standard theory of the congregations,[32] as it still is. It was, indeed, a direct attempt to systematize congregational piety on the assumption of the timeless God. It keeps Father, Son, and Spirit in the same row and so stays close to liturgical use of the triune name and to the linear past, present, and future of baptismal and eucharistic life. But it was nevertheless as much a compromise with Hellenic deity as subordinationism; indeed, it was and is the more complete submission, since the whole biblical talk of God is deprived of reference to God himself. None of the three is He. This is not noticed in immediate liturgical and proclamatory experience, but it is immediately noticed upon reflection. At the levels of learned or dogmatic theology, therefore, modalism has always been rejected promptly on its appearance.[33] We hear of only two noteworthy modalist theologians in the ancient church, Paul of Samosata and Sabellius. The details of their thought did not survive; only their names survived as the ancient church's labels for modalism.

Subordinationism appears able to identify at least the biblical "Father" with God himself. Moreover, it had the missionary advantage that it answered directly to late Hellenism's religious need. Since it puts the Father on top and ranks the Son below him—in vertical order, so to speak—it makes the Son (and sometimes the Spirit) just such a middle being between God's eternity and our time as late antiquity longed for.

Wherever Christ is grasped as a halfway entity between the supposedly timeless God and the temporal world, the subordinationist scheme is established. This can be, was, and is done strictly mythologically,[34] with a demi-God descending and ascending. But it is the sophisticated subordinationism inaugurated around 150 A.D. by the so-called Apologists, the famous Logos-christology, which we must describe, since it created the theological system within and against which developed trinitarianism was to be worked out. Christ, said the Apologists, is—almost—God in that "the Logos" is incarnate in him.

However Justin, Theophilus, and the rest derived or invented their Logos concept, what they meant by it is plain. In the Greek philosophical tradition "logos" is at once *discourse* and the *meaningful order* which discourse discloses.[35] If then the universe has such order, this is a *divine* Logos which is both deity's self-revelatory Discourse and the reasonable Order of the cosmos. Just so the Apologists spoke of "the Logos." Moreover, as the divine Reason *in* our world, the Logos could become the Mediator of deity *to* our world, a "second God," and with the intensifying religious anxiety of late antiquity, that is just what happened.[36] With or without dependence on this extra-Christian development, the Apologists paralleled it and made "the Logos" the name of a typical personalized mediator-entity of second-century religiosity, "the next Power after the Father of all, a Son. . . ."[37] Right or wrong, they thought that in all this they were but continuing John's testimony to the Logos who "was in the beginning with God," who "illumined every man," and who came in flesh to make God known (John 1:1–14).

In that the Apologists shared the interpretation of God as the One who grounds all being by negating time, they shared also late antiquity's great problem, this God's distance. If we are to be saved, God must somehow dwell in our world, all agreed. And in the Old Testament, Christians possessed a narrative of his activity in the world. But God has been defined just by his elevation above temporal action. It cannot have been God himself who walked in Adam's garden or shut the door of Noah's ark or talked to Abraham and Moses, for—as Justin asked—how should he "speak to anyone, or be seen by anyone or appear in a particular part of the earth. . . ? Neither Abraham nor Isaac nor Jacob nor any other human saw the Father, the unutterable Lord . . . , but rather that other, who by his will is his Son and the messenger ["angel"] to serve his purpose."[38] An "other God," one step down the hierarchy of being,[39] is needed to bridge the chasm between God and time.

This "other God" is the Logos, the self-manifesting God, "the Angel of the Lord" of the Hebrew Scriptures. Subordination is explicit. The Logos is "called" God, but over against "the Creator of all things, above whom there is no other God," this predication is not literal.[40] The Logos has "come into being," unlike the Father; he is "from" the unnameable and unoriginated Father, and just so is worshiped "after him."[41]

Since God is rational, he has Logos eternally in himself, as his own Rationality.[42] Then when God moves to create, his Logos becomes external to him as the Rationality manifest in creation. Just so, the Logos is also God's Relation to creation, that is, his Revelation. Thus the Logos is the "first originated being" or even simply "first creature,"[43] over against the Father who has no beginning. No distinction is yet made between different ways of deriving from God, so the difference between the Logos and the world can only be stated by adjectives like "first." It is this divine bridge to time that is then present in Jesus, thus, so to speak, anchoring the bridge at our end.[44] For the second God's derivation from the Father, "Son" suggests "born" and "Logos" suggests "uttered"; both appear and combine in the neutral "gone forth." He is "numerically distinct" from the Father, yet not "set off" from him.[45]

Not much has been said of the Spirit, which leads us to a vital point. The Logos theology is *not* the origin of developed trinitarianism; in itself, it is not in fact trinitarian at all.[46] The primal trinitarian naming and liturgical pattern make a temporal structure horizontal to time and inherently triple as time is. The God/Mediator/World scheme is timelessly vertical to time and of itself would posit either a deity of God and his *one* Mediator or of God and infinitely many mediators.[47] The space between God and the temporal world may be thought of either as one space or as indefinitely divisible, but there is no reason to think of two subspaces. In fact, the status of the Spirit was ambiguous in the whole apologetic theology. Since God "*is* Spirit" according to John (4:24), Spirit can be the name of the divine in Christ.[48] But how then is "*the*" Spirit a third? In the trinitarian pattern itself, on the other hand, there is no problem. On the contrary, we have seen that it is precisely in God's self-posit as Spirit that triune Godhead is established.

Insofar as the Apologists were nevertheless trinitarian, sometimes they arbitrarily stacked all three vertically to time,[49] and sometimes they assigned the Spirit his biblical role outside the mediator scheme altogether.[50] What kept them trinitarian was the presence of factors outside their system: the continuing trinitarian life of the church; the developing three-article creedal structure; perhaps the continuing availability and influence of a *picture* by which to imagine God in accord with this creed, the "Jewish-Christian" picture of the Father and the two great angelic Advocates; and churchly critique of the religious and metaphysical basis of subordinationism, from within Christianized Hellenism. We must next note this critique.

The adjectival-relative—"as if"—extension of deity down a spectrum from "real" deity to us is, after all, the very principle of the religion the Apologists wished to replace, and some of the most compromised among them saw this and disclaimed it. Athenagoras,[51] for example, explicitly adopted the Platonist three-level ontology: divine/mediating/material. And he saw the middle realm as the place of myth. But then he used the doctrine of God's utter timelessness to deny divinity altogether to the denizens of the mid-realm,[52] and so was compelled to try—not very successfully—to locate his "Logos" alongside it.

Or again, the *Epistle to Diognetus* deliberately lists the entire set of semidivine entities ("servants . . . or messengers or powers or overseers of earth . . . or heaven . . .") and realms ("fire, air, light, depth, middle") as subject *to* Christ, precisely as to God himself.[53]

The most profound instance of this critique is that of Irenaeus. Irenaeus read and depended upon Justin and has the same mix of language about God,[54] but he nevertheless launched so principled a polemic against the Gnostic systems that it became a polemic against myth in general, against the very notion of a mid-realm between God and creatures.[55] He attacks the whole conception of reality as a descending set of levels each emanating from the next above and especially of the origin of the Son as such an emanation, rejecting the images by which the earlier Apologists grasped this emanation.[56]

God, he says, in fact needs no mediators of his relation to creation, "for this is the prerogative of God most high, to need no other instrument to create all that is; his own Word is enough."[57] That God is, and that he creates all else that is, are unanalyzable givens.[58] And to this sheer givenness of the Creator belong the Son and the Spirit: "God needs none of them [mediator-beings] to do what he predetermined in himself to do, as if he had not his hands. For always (i.e., prior to all "emanations") there are for him the Word and Wisdom, the Son and the Spirit, by whom and in whom he freely and spontaneously does all."[59] Thus there can be no conception of the origin of the Son or the Spirit.[60] Both are simply eternal as God is eternal.[61]

It is coherent with this critique that Irenaeus is far more directly trinitarian than are his teachers. He uses the Logos concept to state the Son's reality in God and to avoid modalism. But his Logos, preexistent or whatever, is never a mere divine offshoot, but is always the historical man Jesus, the Christ.[62] In the context of the Logos theology, this produces such violently paradoxical formulations as "Neither is Christ one person and Jesus another; the Word of God, who is the Savior of all and the ruler of heaven and of earth, who is

Jesus [!], who assumed flesh and was anointed by the Father with the Spirit, was made to be Jesus Christ."[63] It is the history of God's saving work that is the context of his triune reality. Salvation, as Irenaeus proclaims it, is worked only in the totality of God's historical work and in its precise eternally planned sequence and coherence, that is, in God's "economy."[64] In Irenaeus' presentation this economy has exactly the triune temporal structure we have analyzed,[65] and this structure is the location of God's triune reality: "in the substance of his being there is shown forth one God; but there is also according to the economy of our redemption both Son and Father [and Spirit]."[66] Yet Irenaeus is not a modalist for whom God is triune "only" in his temporal work, for it is the history of salvation that is itself eternal in God as the Logos: "the Creator of all things preformed in his Word the disposition of the human race to the Son of God, first preforming fleshly man, that he might be saved by spiritual man. For since the Savior preexisted, it was necessary for what is saved to come into being, that the Savior not be otiose."[67]

In the interplay of all these factors, apologetic theology reached its historical fulfillment in two great figures of the early third century.[68] In the West, Tertullian taught a more creedal and terminological trinitarianism; in the East, Origen taught a more speculative one. Each set the style of his region for centuries to come. Since the crisis will come in the East, we will take Tertullian first.

For Tertullian, Logos theology was not so much the solution of his own religious problems as part of the now available intellectual repertoire, for use on quite a different problem: the Trinity itself, the proper explication of the Christian interpretation of God. For him, the trinitarian rule of faith was already a given.[69] He was moved to trinitarian analysis by a propagandizing explanation of the rule, the modalism urged in Rome by one Praxeas around 190 A.D.[70] He thought this explanation of the creed explained it away, and he set out to refute it and offer a better one. His means were the Logos theology; the standard philosophy of the region, that is, Stoicism; a more direct relation to the Old Testament than his predecessors had; and his own considerable analytical powers. As it turned out, he set the terminology of all subsequent Western analysis: there are in God "three persons" *(personae)*, who are "of one substance" *(unius substantiae)*.

Perhaps because his concerns were more ethical and communal than religious in the usual late-antique sense, Tertullian's interpretation of God was far more biblical than that of the Apologists. He explicitly distinguished the living personal God of Scripture from both the numina of old Roman religion and the abstract deity of Hellenism.[71] In the train of the Apologists, he used the negative predicates, but secondarily and sparingly, preferring the biblical "unique," "true," and "living."[72] So far from using "God" as an adjective, he took it for a proper name.[73] And despite formal adherence to the negative theology and lapses into more conventional caution, at the height of his christological passion he can defiantly affirm the "humiliations and sufferings of God,"[74] in full knowledge of the offense to what is also for him the only sensible theology. "What is unworthy for God is needed for me. . . . The Son of God has died; it is to be believed just because it is unlikely."[75] Even the unchangeability axiom could be defied: because nothing is equal to God, so that he has no effective opposite, "God can be changed into all things and yet remain as he is."[76]

Appropriately, Tertullian's use of the Logos concept is closer to the Old Testament's—or Ignatius'—notion of God's creative *Utterance* than to the Apologists' cosmic Rationality. Insofar as he incorporates the Greek notion of Logos as divine Reason, he interprets it as God's inner discourse: "God, like us, is rational by silently thinking through and disposing with himself what is about to be uttered."[77] God planned the world and its history in interior discourse. Then he *spoke*, "Let there be light," and this was the birth of the Word.[78] Thus, after trying several Latin formulas as his equivalent for the Greek *logos*, Tertullian settled on *sermo*, which denotes precisely the vocal utterance.[79]

For the rest, Tertullian's Logos theology was as subordinationist as any; perhaps, owing to his analytic clarity, it was more bluntly so than most. But the creed, not the Logos theology, set the structure of his trinitarianism.[80] Within this structure, the Logos theology served two purposes, to both of which its subordinationism was actually irrelevant. It served as theory of how one self-equal substance could be two or three something-or-others.[81] And it served as an explanation of how God could simultaneously be "invisible" and "impassible"—that is, all that people said a proper God had to be—and be seen, crucified, and all Tertullian believed God in fact was. The Father was the one, the Son the other.[82]

Tertullian's own trinitarian concern was to show how God's "monarchy" and "economy" could be simultaneously preserved.[83] "Monarchy" was his opponents' slogan for the abstract oneness of God as such, which Tertullian made mean instead the uniqueness and self-consistency of God's *rule*, of his divine *work*.[84] Tertullian himself adapted "economy" to be a term of trinitarian analysis. In Irenaeus it meant the historical unfolding of God's saving work; Tertullian uses it for God's own inner self-disposition in this saving history.[85] It is "the economy . . . which disposes the unity into trinity."[86] Plainly it is theological interpretation of the three-step creed that is Tertullian's task; *both* the one and three are those of God's reality in saving history.

For the three to which God's economy "disposes" him, Tertullian used *personae*, establishing the word for all subsequent Western theology. *Persona* had been first the actor's mask through which he spoke, then the role the actor thus played, and by Tertullian's time was the everyday term for the human individual, established in his individuality by his social role, by his speaking and responding.[87] The immediate background of the word's trinitarian use was an established exegetical use.[88] The Logos was considered by ancient theology as the agent of all revelation; therefore when Scripture attributes speech to the Father or the Spirit this was said to be the Son speaking "in the person" (*ex persona*) of the Father or the Spirit. Exegetically, Tertullian was thus accustomed to the three, in their distinction from one another, being called "persons."[89] The step to use in trinitarian analysis was apparently taken before Tertullian; it was in any case a short one.[90]

Tertullian's assertion of three *personae* in God is thus the assertion against modalism that the role distinctions, the relations of address and response found in Scripture between the Father and Jesus and the Spirit, establish reality in God, just as such relations do among human individuals.[91] Tertullian's cases of the distinction of "persons"[92] all come down to the narrative over-againstness of Father, Jesus, and Spirit in Scripture. They are three in that they speak to and about one another[93] in such scriptural incidents as Jesus' baptism. They are three because they have three mutually recognized proper names.[94] Also the inner-trinitarian eternal roles are defined by the roles in saving history; when God said, "Let us make man," "he spoke, in the unity of the trinity, with the Son, who was to put on man, and with the Spirit, who was to sanctify man, as with ministers and councillors."[95]

The unity of the three persons is conceived on the model of the Christian community, in which mutual identification makes one reality, "one body," and on the model of the profound Stoic conception of organic unity.[96] In the case of God such unities are taken to the limit. The three in God are perfect community and perfect organism, so as to be only one God. This perfection of unity is expressed by calling the three one "substance,"[97] to which concept we must now turn.

Substantia came both from everyday speech and from the technical vocabulary of Stoic philosophy in Latin.[98] In the latter it functioned as the translation of several Greek terms but had its own Latin weight; for each real thing, the "substance" is the reliably real underlying and persisting foundation of its shifting states and appearances, conceived on the model of the sheer *stuff* that persists from, for example, a block of stone, through the statue made of it, through the statue's broken pieces, and so on for as long as some continuous identity can be ascertained. It can be used interchangeably with "body" (*corpus*), for what is simply *there*, before and immune to all reflection. According to Tertullian, there is a specific divine substance, Spirit, understood in thoroughly biblical fashion, which in the dynamic relations of the persons establishes both their unity and the reality of each. He can say, "the Spirit is the body of the Word"[99]—and similarly for the Father.[100]

It was almost solely the terminology thus specified that shaped subsequent Western tradition.[101] Tertullian's subordinationism was both separable from the rest of his thought and uncongenial to the Western church, which in its unspeculative loyalty to congregational tradition erred rather toward modalism. And his Roman-Stoic conceptuality was soon, under increasing Platonist influence, found materialist and anthropomorphic—and in my opinion many good beginnings were therewith jettisoned.

The resultant terminology—*persona* used as by Tertullian and *substantia* detached from any particular philosophical background—was useful both for good and for bad. It gave the Western church language with which to get on with its daily proclamatory and disciplinary business, 175 years before this urgent necessity was filled in the East. But in its conceptual blandness it also served to obscure the very real religious and intellectual problems posed by the Christian identification of God. These were to be faced in the East.

That event was prepared by the first truly great thinker and scholar of Christian history, Origen of Alexandria, who carried subordinationist trinitarianism to its unstable perfection and created a way of thinking that dominated the Eastern church for the remainder of its theologically creative history. Though he was a far greater theologian than Tertullian, his role in our special story is so much that of the fulfiller of already described tendencies that our treatment can be brief. Two great aspects of his work may be simply noted here, for future reference. He was the creator of hermeneutically self-conscious biblical exegesis; from him the Eastern church learned to search the Scriptures with consistent and explicit method. And he was the first great christologian after John the Evangelist, the first to do all theology as meditation on and analysis of the reality of Christ.

Origen's God the Father is Hellenic deity in purest form: sheer Mind, utterly removed from the temporal material world, utterly undifferentiated, and just so unknowable in himself.[102] The unknowability of God is not an accident resulting from the weakness of our comprehension, but his ontological difference from other reality.[103] And this difference is identical with the difference between the temporal and the timeless.[104] God is knowable only as Ground of his works, by the intuition of *nous*; even the exegesis of Scripture is fixed into this scheme by the doctrine of allegory, which makes the true sense of Scripture a hidden sense to which the mind must penetrate.[105]

Accordingly, Origen's entire soteriological concern is for mediation of the knowledge of God.[106] He perfects the apologetic theology of mediation by consistent and fully elaborated use of a fundamental concept of late-antique, and especially Alexandrian, religion and philosophy: image *(eikon)*. Plato had already encountered the problem of mediating the timeless divine and the temporal world and had found the possibility of mediation in the aesthetic category of "imitation." A statue or painting is not its archetype and yet is nothing else than its archetype; an *image* is thus midway between being and nonbeing.[107] Just so, this entire world can be grasped as the image of its eternal Ground. The world is not its own ground but also is not other than it; it is like an artist's imitation of a model.[108] Under the pressure of later antiquity's more desperate need for mediation, middle Platonism replaced Plato's two levels with a plural hierarchy of levels of being and grasped each intermediate level as image of reality above and archetype of reality below.[109] For this tradition, "image" thus comes to be the chief category for mediation of time and eternity. As archetype, an intermediary image is the proximate ground of inferior reality. As image of superior reality, it mediates to inferior reality a knowledge of the Ground beyond; in that we see God's image, we truly see God, yet his unknowability in himself is preserved. Origen is this tradition's great Christian member.[110]

As *the* Image of God, the Son has his own Ground in the Father and is in turn the Ground of all other being.[111] Just so, he is God's permanent revelation: "In the Word, since he is . . . the Image of the unseen God, we see the Father who begot him; he who looks into the Image can intuit also the Archetype of the Image, that is, the Father."[112] And precisely in that we know God in the Word, we are ourselves fulfilled as images of God and so perfected in our proper being. As God reflects himself in the Image and the "images of the Image,"[113] the world is created. As creatures know God, each in the next image up, the world is saved.[114]

God the Son is "God's Wisdom . . . substantially subsisting";[115] in him the "powers and forms of all that is to be created" are present.[116] Just so, the Son is the revelation of God's intention to the creatures when they exist, and so is "Word" as well as "Wisdom."[117] The Son's birth from the Father is without beginning, even in the abstract; it is an "eternal . . . generation, as radiance is born from a light."[118] The problem of a category for the Son's "birth" is solved for all following theology: in that God knows himself, there is God as the object of God's knowledge, and in that this knowledge is communicative, God-the-Object goes out from God.[119] Conversely, the Son subsists in and only in that he contemplates the Father;[120] he *is* the Father's self-reflection.

Also, the Spirit is eternal, given from God without beginning.[121] And the problem of the trinitarian place of the Spirit is ingeniously solved. The Spirit's work is sanctification, his sphere is the church;[122] Origen includes the church's special reality in his mediation system. He conceives the work of Father, Son, and Spirit as three concentric circles, along the line of mediation between God and us, as an inverted stepped cone. The Father gives being to all beings; the Son gives the knowledge of God to all those beings capable of knowledge; the Spirit gives the holiness in which such knowledge is fulfilled to those among rational beings who are to be saved.[123] Both the downward mediation of being and the upward mediation of fulfillment are thus essentially triune.[124]

Thus Origen's system is fully trinitarian in its own way. God has two mediators[125] for the universal and particular of his relation to the world. It is likely that the "Jewish Christian" image of the two seraphims, spiritualized of course, played an important part in shaping Origen's vision. At least he regularly refers to it at key points.[126] Origen can speak in a way not to be achieved generally for a century; it is "the blessed . . . *Trinity"* as such which is "the good God and benign universal Father."[127] From this point of view, all three are definitely on the God-side of the ontological divide: "All that is said of Father, Son, and Spirit must be understood apart from all temporality."[128]

But the system is also fully subordinationist. Precisely in order to be the image of God that reveals God to us, the Son must be intermediate, true God with respect to us, but not with respect to the Father, substantially all that the Father is, but "circumscribed" to our capacity.[129] He is "the image of the invisible God and insofar God, but is not *so* God as is the one of whom Christ himself said 'that they may know you the only true God'—thus, for example, he is the image of goodness, but not unalterably good as is the Father."[130] Nor is, within Origen's system, the assertion of the Son's eternity quite the ontological decision it would be elsewhere, for Origen asserts the eternity of creation also[131]—though not, to be sure, of the present creation. As to the Spirit, Origen was able simply to call him a "creature."[132] Indeed, both Son and Spirit can be called God precisely in that they are in their invisibility unlike "the other creatures."[133] "Thus the power of the Father is greater than that of the Son and the Holy Spirit, and that of the Son greater than that of the Spirit."[134] From this point of view, deity is an adjective permitting degrees; the Son and Spirit are "related by nature" to the "other rational beings," and all together are more divine than nonrational beings.[135] As the first images of God, the Son and Spirit have place in an indefinite hierarchy of imaging, which extends through them to "the images of the Image," who have "the same relation to the Word . . . as he has to God himself."[136]

The Arian Crisis

The Origenist system[137] was unstable, since the initial mere compromise between biblical and Hellenic interpretation of God still lay at its heart. In historical particular, it could not stand the question "Well, which *is* the Logos, Creator or creature?" The secret of subordinationist trinitarianism, perfected by Origen, was the posit of an unbroken continuity of being from the great God, through the Logos, the Spirit, and other "spiritual" beings, down to temporal beings. Across this beautiful spectrum the biblical radical distinction of Creator from creature could only make an ugly slash somewhere. But the intense and open study of Scripture, which was the other great achievement of Origenism itself, had sooner or later to pose the Creator-creature difference inescapably.

The intellectual and religious instability of Origenism was also a confessional instability of the Eastern church, for at the turn of the third and fourth centuries, the great bishoprics and professorships of the East were almost all occupied by Origenists of one shade or another, from a left wing of those most drawn by Origen's intellectual respectability, to a right wing most drawn by his christological passion. Eusebius of Caesarea, who was to be the Constantinean Empire's great propagandist bishop, can represent the left; Athanasius himself, in his pre-Nicene writings, the right.

Eusebius' interpretation of God the Father is a perfect case of uncritical Christian adoption of Hellenic theology; the Father is "above origin and before the first and more original than the monad and beyond every category—unutterable, ungraspable, unknowable."[138] Eusebius knows of this agreement; all men, he thinks, agree about the "first" God.[139] "God" is, moreover, explicitly an adjective used analogically at various descending levels of the imaging of the divine: the Father is called "God" "literally," the Son "appropriately but not properly," "deserving" the adjective "more" than the other images of God—that is, more than we or the angels—by the precision of his imaging.[140]

The descending images are needed because God's involvement in the world of time, including the history of salvation, is contrary to proper deity.[141] In order, therefore, that lower beings might not lack communion with God, he "instituted the divine power of the First-Begotten as a sort of middle thing," so that those too weak to tolerate God himself might have a "second" God, "tailored" to their weakness.[142]

Following Origen, Eusebius insists that the Logos is a distinct reality over against the Father. Thus when he uses the analogy of a light and its ray, he quickly amends it: "But the ray is not apart from the light, whereas the son stands in his own right and in his own way beside the Father, having reality of his own kind."[143] Eusebius needs this distinctness to secure the Son's ability to mediate between God and us, and he can see no other way to secure it than to make the Son ontologically, though not temporally, later than the Father, and therefore less godly than God "himself."[144] Eusebius' basic ontological line is between "originating" being and "originated," and the Son is of the latter.[145] And yet he is God— of a sort.[146] Eusebius, plainspoken subordinationist: "[the Son] is greater than any angelic nature, but less than the First Cause."[147]

Athanasius' pre-Nicene thought projects an equally Origenist vision of reality—and, indeed, he studied Eusebius! The Logos is the Image of God;[148] we are the images of the Logos; and our salvation is the contemplation of God in the Logos.[149] The descending imaging is, moreover, needed because the Father is in himself invisible.[150] Athanasius can attack polytheism and superstition with all the weapons of the Hellenic Enlightenment, as confident as Eusebius that God is "by nature bodiless . . . and invisible and ungraspable."[151]

But Athanasius finds in Origen's vision and dialectics very different possibilities than does Eusebius. His Logos is not located on a middle ontological level between God and man. On the one hand, when he calls the Logos "God" he does so altogether without qualification; affirming the doctrine that the Son has his being *from* the Father, he draws no subordinationist conclusions.[152] And it is Origen's doctrine of the Son's coeternity that enables this: Father and Son define one another in deity.[153] On the other hand, the Logos is simply identified with Jesus Christ, even the Logos from whom mankind fell was "the true Word of the Father, our Savior, Christ."[154] When Athanasius must speak of the not-yet-incarnate Logos, he identifies him as *the one who will be* Christ.[155] In consequence of both these aspects, Athanasius is consistent in identifying God himself not by ontological prerogatives—as Eusebius' "unoriginated"—but by his character as "the Father of our Lord."[156]

Origenist—or other—subordinationism's inevitable breakdown was triggered by the students and other disciples of Lucian of Antioch.[157] Lucian's theology is not well known. In the last decades of the third century and the first of the fourth, he was a great teacher in the style of Origen, a martyr, and the founder of Antioch's scholarly fame. His students learned a methodical exegesis of Scripture more devoted to the literal sense than Origen's, and therefore more likely to intrude the dangerous Creator/creature language. They learned also a less mystically heated and more coolly analytical—"Aristotelian"—Platonism, amenable to such commonsensicalities as that each thing is itself and not another. This made Origen's spectrum of being look more like a set of steps than a glissando, and so emphasized its subordinationism: if the Logos is a distinct entity only a very, very little bit different from God, then he is, said the Lucianists, in fact *different*.[158]

The struggle began among the Egyptian clergy.[159] The priest of an Alexandrian parish, a decidedly second-rate Lucianist named Arius, attacked the Origenist right wing's tendency to the old paradox christology with its flat-out attribution of divine eternity to the Son.[160] Since the attack touched the bishop, Alexander, a synod of Egyptian bishops shortly deposed Arius and a few sympathizers.

Thereupon Arius appealed to the old-school tie. Leaving Egypt, he and his fellow rebels sought and found place with the most notable of the Lucianists, Bishop Eusebius of Nicomedia. Eusebius launched a correspondence campaign among the Eastern bishops to have Arius restored to office. Alexander responded. A general uproar ensued, which can only be explained by the theological development being ripe for it.

What Arius and his friends were concerned about is explicit and clear in the very first document of the conflict, Arius' appeal to Eusebius of Nicomedia. As Arius understands it, those who attribute to the Son coeternity with the Father must regard the Son either as some sort of emergent from *within* the Father's being or as a *parallel* unoriginated being.[161] Both are termed "blasphemies."

For Arius, and for the whole Lucianist group to which he appealed, and indeed for all the more left-wing disciples of Origen, there were only two identifying characteristics of God. First, God is "unoriginated." As we have seen, the theology deriving from the Apologists did not differentiate between possible different ways of having an origin, and so had "*un*originated" as the only alternative to "originated." Left-wing Origenism made this catchall negative definitive of deity.[162] Second, God is altogether devoid of internal differentiation.[163]

For Arius, therefore, to say that the Son is "co-unoriginated," or anything of the sort, posits two "co-gods," while to say that the Son is an emergent from within the Father introduces differentiation into even the Father, that is, denies that there is any real God at all.[164] Arius therefore teaches: that "the Son is not unoriginated, nor is he in any way a part of the Unoriginated."[165]

It it plain that what moves Arius is the late-Hellenic need to escape time, to become utterly dominant. If we are to be saved, Arius supposes, there must be some reality entirely uninvolved with time, which has no origin of any sort and whose continuity is undifferentiated and uninterrupted. Just so, it is because Christ is involved with time that he will not do as *really* God: "How can the Logos be God, who sleeps like a man and weeps and suffers?"[166] It had long been decided, against the modalists, that the longed-for absolute Timeless and Impassible One cannot be a divine essence other than Father, Son, and Spirit; then it must be the Father. Very early the Arians put

their case in two sentences: "As the *monad*, and the *Source* of
all things, God is *before* all things. Therefore he is also before
the Son."[167] All other considerations must be sacrificed to this
logic and the religious need behind it.

If the Son is neither unoriginated nor originated by emergence from the Father, it follows, according to Arius, that "the
Son has a beginning."[168] At this point Arius' bishop, Alexander, became alarmed,[169] for once the new study of Scripture,
as promoted by Lucian himself, had freshly impressed the distinction between Creator and creature, to say without further
ado that the Son is "originated" is to call him a creature. And
that is exactly what Arius sometimes did. In the statement that
Arius and his fellow exiles first sent out from Nicomedia, we
read: "We confess . . . that God has originated an only
Son . . . , God's perfect creature."[170] Alexander equally insisted
on "the great gap between the unoriginated Father and the
creatures," including any created pure spirits,[171] but in irrec-
oncilable contrast with the Arians, he put the Logos on the far
side: since the Logos is acknowledged creative, he cannot
therefore "be of the same nature as creatures."[172]

To be sure, the notion of "creature" was still ambiguous in
learned theology. Indeed, keeping it ambiguous was in the
interest of all who wanted to preserve the Origenist settlement;
thus in the letter to Alexander even Arius wrote, ". . . God's
perfect creature, but not as one of the creatures"—whatever
that meant.[173] But "creation" has its function against the horizon of time, and here there was an unambiguous Arian statement around which the controversy was to be conducted:
"There was once when he [the Logos] was not."[174] In the direction of the transcendence from which we come, and into
which we are to return, the way, according to the Arians, leads
beyond what happens in time with Christ to a God who is not
yet the Father of the Son,[175] who is a sheer Unoriginate, above
all differentiation and relation.[176] As we climb back up the ladder of being, the Logos, so long as he is above us, is God for
us; but he is not God in himself.[177] The great thinker of later
Arianism (350–380), Eunomius, was finally to draw the reli-

gious conclusion: the last goal is precisely to transcend the Revealer and see God as he does.[178]

In the long conflict the opposition to Arius was to be carried above all by Athanasius, Alexander's adviser and then his successor as bishop.[179] He attacked precisely the Arian vision of God as not that of the gospel. If God is not intrinsically Father of the Son, he is not intrinsically Father, for "father" is relational.[180] But being fatherly defines the God Christians worship; therefore he can no more be God without the Son than light can be without shining.[181] It is Origen's doctrine of the eternal generation of the Son—that the origin of the Son from the Father is not in time at all—that is here adapted.[182] The very *being* of the Father would be "unfinished" without the Son; God's "goodness" is that he is Father; his "truth" is the Son; and the Son cannot be a creature willed by the Father because the Son *is* the Father's will.[183] It is not too much to say that, for Athanasius, *what* the Son reveals about God is exactly *that* God is his Father.

Since relation to us, as the Father of our Lord, is internal to God's being, there is no need for bridge-beings between God and us. The great religious need of late antiquity is not filled by the gospel; it is abolished. Once Athanasius sees this clearly, he is free to label the adjectival and graded use of "God" as what it is: "polytheism, for since they [the Arians] call [the Son] God, because it is so written, but do not call him proper to the Father's being, they introduce a plurality of . . . forms of divine being."[184] But assimilating created beings to God is the very principle of non-Christian religion: "This is the characteristic of the Greeks, to introduce a creature into the Trinity."[185] The middle realm is gone altogether: "If Son, not creature; if creature, not Son."[186]

In Athanasius' mature thought, a mainstay of his argument was the canonical command to baptize in the trinitarian name.[187] This command establishes "Father-and-Son-and-Holy-Spirit" as the Christian's God, and the Arians have not challenged this. But if they then call the Son or the Spirit a creature, they bring a creature into God and are embarked on polytheism: "Your baptism . . . is not wholly into deity, for a creature is mixed in; . . . like the Greeks you name creature and creator God together."[188] In rich variation, argument from the one but triple name into which we are baptized was to become basic for all later anti-Arian argument.[189] With it Gregory of Nazianzus, ca. 360 A.D., tied all the anti-Arian arguments into one neat package: "If he [the Logos] is not to be worshiped . . . , how can he unite me to God by baptism? But if he is to be worshiped, how is he not God?"[190] The point, we may note, applies fully as well to halfhearted christologies of the present.

Nicaea and Constantinople

Driven by equal and opposite ultimate concerns, the churchmen of the eastern Empire therefore fell upon one another when Arius blurted out "when he was not." And just at this point the first Christian emperor assumed power. Constantine came as an agent of universal peace, dreaming of the *pax Romana* restored by the new religion of love, and he found the bishops in a brawl, the most learned in the front. After initial failed efforts to restore peace, he commanded a general council of the bishops of the eastern Empire to meet at Nicaea in 325, in succession of the earlier Egyptian council.

Those who attended found themselves at the first great meeting of ecumenical Christianity, in a world suddenly turned from persecution to supplication. Understandably, they were in no more mood for disturbers of unity than was Constantine. They confirmed the condemnation of Arius and deposed his more intransigent supporters. And they produced a rule for talk about Christ which excluded Arius and his immediate followers but which all others—even Eusebius of Nicomedia—contrived to sign. Into a typical three-article liturgical creed, they inserted four theological explications: Christ, they said, is "out of the being of the Father": "*true* God of true God," "begotten not created," and "*homoousios* (of one being) with the Father."[191] This is the decree of Nicaea, the first deliberately created doctrine.

It is of first importance that the Nicene decree is an expanded congregational creed. It is daily trinitarian liturgical naming of the gospel's God, and interpreting of three-arrowed time by his particular deity, which is affirmed and then protectively analyzed by the inserted theological phrases.

"Out of the being of the Father"[192] affirms just that origin of Christ within God's own self which Arius most feared. The phrase says that the Son is not an entity originated outside God by God's externally directed choice, that he is not in any sense a creature. And it says that there *is* differentiation within God, that the relation to the Son is an "internal relation" in the Father,[193] a relation necessary to his being God the Father. *To be God is to be related.* With that the fathers contradicted the main principle of Hellenic theology.

"Begotten and not created" makes exactly that distinction between two ways of being originated from God, the lack of which enabled the subordinationist glissando from God himself, who is unoriginated, to us, who are originated, through the Son, who is a bit of each. On the contrary, we are "created," the Son is "begotten," and these are just two different things.[194] Nobody claimed to know exactly what "begotten" meant in this connection, and yet a tremendous assertion is made: there is a way of being *begun*, of receiving one's being, which is proper to Godhead itself. To be God is not only to give being, it is also to receive being. And there went the rest of Plato.

"*True* God of true God" prohibits all use of the analogy principle in calling Jesus "God." He is plain God, not qualified God. In ontology-shaking effect, the insertion of "true" prohibits the relative, adjectival use of "God," or at least it prohibits it of the Son, which is the only place Christians would have used it.

And finally there is the famous and fateful "*homoousios* with the Father." The history of the word *homoousios* was checkered.[195] Its first theological use was by Gnostics, for the mythic emergences of their different divine entities. From these it spread into subtheological Christian use, probably for more or

less modalist expressions. In a brief third-century clash between the bishops of Alexandria and Rome, it appears as a
translation of Tertullian's *unius substantiae*, which was ill regarded in Alexandria for its materialist flavor. Origen used the
word, but rarely, to say that the Son had all the same essential
characters as the Father, but on another ontological level.[196]

We do not know how or why this came to be Nicaea's big
word. Perhaps it was introduced precisely by Arius' negative
use simply to contradict him. Arius had said, "The Son . . . is
not *homoousios* with [the Father]" to reject Western-type trinitarianism or any notion of Father and Son being two by division of one substance.[197]

The bishops seemingly did not have any one meaning in
mind when they used *homoousios* affirmatively. Constantine's
Western advisers at Nicaea,[198] thinking in Latin, no doubt took
homoousios as a perfect equivalent of Tertullian's "of one substance" and had no further problem. For those who thought
in Greek it was not so simple. Did *homoousios* mean the same
as it did in Origen? The most ardent anti-Arians, such as
Athanasius, suspected it might, and that it might therefore be
a poor guard against subordinationism; they were for a time
wary in their use of it. Did it mean that Father and Son both
had all the characteristics of Godhead, whatever these are?
Then are there not two (or three) Gods? Or did it, in more
Aristotelian fashion, mean that Father and Son were numerically one actual entity? But how then could modalism be
avoided? The Lucianists feared modalism could *not* be avoided,
and when one of the chief Nicene anti-Arians, Marcellus of
Ancyra, turned out in fact to be a modalist, they had a horror
example ever after.[199]

Yet so much was clear: *homoousios* meant that Arius was a
heretic, since he denied it.[200] Contradicting his contradiction:
there is only one divine being, and both Father and Son have
it. Whatever it means to be God, pure and simple, Christ is,[201]
and that suffices to make the needed and revolutionary point:
Christ is not at all the sort of halfway entity that normal religion
needs and provides to mediate time and eternity. He is not a

divine teacher or example, a personal savior, a mediator of grace, or any other of the beloved semigods of standard Western culture-religion. He is constitutive of God, not merely revelatory of him—or if one develops a whole theology of revelation, then being revealed in Christ is itself constitutive of deity.

Abrupt and almost instinctive though they were, the Nicene phrases make the decisive differentiation between Christian and other interpretations of God, then and now. Proclamation of a God or salvation they do not fit cannot be the gospel, however otherwise religious or beneficial. The Arian incident was the decisive crisis to date, and the Nicene Creed the decisive victory to date, in Christianity's self-identification. The gospel—Nicaea finally said unequivocally—provides no mediator of our ascent to a timeless and therefore distant God; it rather proclaims a God whose own deity is not separable from a figure of our temporal history and who therefore is not and never has been timeless and distant from us.

The bishops were not clearly aware of what they had said with this creed, except that Arius had gone too far. When they went home, they slowly became aware that they had overturned the whole Origenist settlement. Then the real fight began, to last for sixty years.

Subordinationist trinitarianism had not yet undone itself from within; it had only been denounced in a crude version. A variety of moves could seemingly yet be tried to combine the glissando of being with the difference between Creator and creature. In the next forty years each such move would produce a new creedal proposal and a new alignment against Athanasius. Moreover, the Nicene dogma was incomplete; what about the Spirit? So soon as the matter was noted—in Egypt again—a whole new spectrum of disputes came into being.

The Lucianists began the new struggle,[202] refusing to take Nicaea as the last word and working for possession of the bishoprics and for ecumenical acceptance of a more "moderate" creed. The lineup shifted with each new theological attempt. At one end of the spectrum were two groups: Athanasius with his followers, and the Western bishops.[203] The Western bishops stuck to Tertullian's formula, never quite understood the Easterners' problems, and supported Athanasius when they dared.[204] It took some daring, for after Nicaea the anti-Nicene reaction usually contrived to look like the peace-loving middle of the road, and so to secure imperial support. At the other end of the spectrum were actual Arians, some willing to be called that and others not, sporadically recruited from the Origenist middle. In between were the majority of Eastern churchmen, from those like Eusebius of Caesarea on the left to near-Nicenes on the right. Their common purpose was to preserve the traditional Origenist theology of the East. But once the challenge of the *homoousios* was there, their ground proved slippery, and the left wing constantly slid into practically Arian positions.

After initial hesitation, Athanasius found he could use *homoousios* as a slogan for his vision of God, to mean that the Father and the Son (and the Spirit) *together* make the one reality of God. The Godhead of the Son is not "by participation" in *another's* Godhead; rather, "the fact that there is the son is a proper characteristic of the Father's being."[205] Indeed, Athanasius' preferred expression is that the Son—and the Spirit—are "proper to the Father's reality."[206] Thus *homoousios* denotes a resemblance of the Son to the Father that is not merely the infinite degree of resemblance between two things, but rather means that "the Son is the *same one, by* resemblance."[207] *Homoousios*, Athanasius explains, is the logical product of *homoousios*, "having the same characteristics," and *ek tes physeos*, "from the being of."[208] Moreover, that the Father and the Son have the same characteristics follows from their having the one being, not vice versa.[209] And so finally, "eternal and one is the deity in the Trinity; and one the glory thereof."[210] *Homoousios* of the Father and the Son means *both* that the differentiation of the Son from the Father is internal to *what* it means to be God[211] and that the differentiation is internal to the concrete singularity of the *one who is* all that it means to be God.[212]

It is the Trinity as such—and not the Father as such—who is God. In the judgment of Athanasius' contemporaries, this insight was his great theological achievement.[213] And whatever sundry bishops at Nicaea may have meant by *homoousios*, it is with this significance that the word lives in churchly history. The various anti-Nicene coalitions, in clear contrast, took the Father by himself as "really" God, and the Son, next down on the spectrum of being, as very closely—perhaps even "altogether"—*assimilated* to God.[214] Confused as the terminologies were, the issue was and is simple and vital to faith. The issue is not so much the "status" of Jesus as about who and what is God himself.

Anti-homoousian slogans waxed and waned.[215] None quite worked; a new one would be tried. The final result of the anti-Nicene movement was the discrediting of subordinationism, by the destruction in its cause of the confessional unity of the Eastern church. For example, in Antioch just before 360 there was a complete denominational system: a congregation of out-and-out Arians, a congregation of sophisticated Arians, the official church with a Eusebian bishop, a pro-Nicene group that had submitted to the bishop but also held its own meetings, and a separate congregation of intransigent Nicaeans.[216]

As the weary creed-making went on, many not originally of Athanasius' party began to see that the vision of God evoked by *homoousios*—as used by Athanasius—was theirs too.[217] What was needed for the East was an explanation of how this could work, of how one might indeed say that Father and Son are one God, and that this is not a matter of their being God on different levels, without thereby falling into modalism,[218] that is, how one could hold to Origen's decisive insight that Father, Son, and Spirit are indeed *three* in God, otherwise than by ranking them ontologically.

Such a theory was finally provided in the 370s by a brilliant new generation of bishops and teachers, again schooled by Origen but using his dialectic to overcome his subordinationism. The most powerful thinkers among these were "the Cappadocians": Basil the Great, primate of Cappadocia; Basil's

brother, Gregory of Nyssa, and his protégé, Gregory Nazianzus. Analysis of their thought itself belongs in the next chapter.
Here a crude characterization will suffice: the Cappadocians
took Origen's three hypostases and his real distinctions among
them, in Origen a ladder reaching vertically from God to time,
and tipped it on its side, to make a structure horizontal to time
and reaching from point to point in God. Of what was for
Origen the structure joining God and time, they made a structure of God's own reality. Just such a stroke was what was
needed to enable general acceptance of Nicaea's dogma.

Moreover, the Cappadocians finally discredited subordinationism intellectually by starkly stating the contradiction which
it indeed contained and which had led to the chaos of parties.
If subordinationists say the Son and the Spirit are *inferior* deity,
they assert a plurality of sorts of deity, that is, they are poly-
theists. If they say Son and Spirit are simply *not* God, they
must stop worshiping them or worship creatures; either way,
they again have defected to paganism.[219] The entire principle
of mediating degrees of divinity, which had been traditional
for centuries, is now clearly perceived and rejected: "To com-
pose the Trinity of Great and Greater and Greatest, as if of
Light and Beam and Sun . . . , makes a 'ladder of deity' that
will not bring us into heaven but out of it."[220]

Emperor Theodosius I, determined like his predecessors to
reunite the church, summoned yet another council at Constantinople in 381.[221] It was a council of Basil's followers, and it
succeeded where all before had failed. This council proclaimed
the Nicene confession as official confession of the East by affirming yet another regional baptismal creed that in Nicene use
had been enriched with the Nicene phrases,[222] and it added an
affirmation of the full deity of the Spirit,[223] with insertions into
the third article: ". . . the Lord, the Giver of life, proceeding
from the Father, worshiped and glorified with the Father and
the Son. . . ." In this article, the word *homoousios* was itself
avoided, so as not to start the struggle about terminology
again.

The article on the Spirit completed the trinitarian dogma.

Since the Spirit was, on the subordinationist hierarchy, one more step from God than the Logos, affirmation of his full Godhead marked final rejection of the whole subordinationist principle. Moreover, the assertion that the Spirit "proceeds from the Father," paired with the "begetting" of the Logos, finally wrenched the whole discourse about inner-divine origins from the mythic associations the Apologists gave it. The "begetting" of the Logos was easily, and by itself almost inevitably, understood congruently with the late-antique mediation of Eternity and time by a mythic mid-realm that emerges from real deity and moves just far enough in our direction to make contact. Indeed, it was to provide a Christian version of this mid-realm that the Apologists had introduced the "begetting" terminology in the first place, and subordinationism of all brands was the attempt to maintain it in this function. But just so, subordinationism could not imagine what another sort of inner-divine originating, that of the Spirit, could be for. To assert, as a meaningful and necessary gospel-affirmation, a second kind of inner-divine origin, "proceeding," was to embark on the enterprise of putting all the Apologetic and Origenist language and dialectics to a new use—that is, on Athanasius' and the Cappadocians' project. Thus it was on Constantinople's assertions about the Spirit that the mildly Origenist middle of the road finally divided into those who entered the reconstituted ecumenical church and those who continued in waning opposition or sectarianism.[224]

One step remains in the story of the Nicene doctrine. In 451, long after these battles were over, the Council of Chalcedon formally proclaimed both the creed of Nicaea and the creed of Constantinople as dogma for the whole church, East and West.[225] Since then, the Constantinopolitan creed—usually and somewhat misleadingly called "the Nicene Creed"—has come to dominate liturgical use, since it contains the phrases for the Spirit. Both creeds together are actually the dogmatic document. It has since been an ecumenical rule of all talk in the Christian church: in all three temporal directions of our relation to Jesus Christ, we have unsurpassably to do with

God, and just by this circumstance our God differs from the culture-God of Western civilization, even in his Christianized versions.

NOTES

1. The following paragraphs depend on the standard histories: Jane Ellen Harrison, *Prolegomena to the Study of Greek Religion* (Cambridge: Cambridge University Press, 1903), esp. chaps. 1, 6, 7; Martin P. Nilsson, *A History of Greek Religion,* trans. F. J. Fielden (Oxford: Clarendon, 1925); Martin P. Nilsson, "Die Griechen," in *Lehrbuch der Religionsgeschichte,* ed. Chantepie de la Saussaye (Tübingen: J. C. B. Mohr, 1925), 2:281–417; Ulrich von Wilamowitz-Moellendorf, *Der Glaube der Hellenen* (Berlin: Weidmann, 1932). The interpretation is heavily influenced by Ulrich Mann, *Vorspiel des Heils* (Stuttgart: Klett, 1962).

2. Sophocles *Oedipus the King* 1528–30.

3. Aristotle *Metaphysics* 1051b29–30.

4. Werner Jaeger, *The Theology of the Early Greek Philosophers* (Oxford: Clarendon, 1947).

5. Aristotle *Physics* 203b7ff.

6. E.g., Maximus of Tyre *Who Is God?* 11.9d; Plutarch *Isis and Osiris* 54.

7. See Eberhard Jüngel, *Zum Ursprung der Analogie bei Parmenides und Heraklit* (Berlin: de Gruyter, 1964), esp. p. 29.

8. K. von Fritz, "The Function of Nous," *CP* 38 (1943): 79–93; 40 (1945): 223–42; 41 (1946): 12–34; Werner Marx, *The Meaning of Aristotle's "Ontology"* (The Hague: Nijhoff, 1954), pp. 8–29.

9. See Hans Jonas, *Gnosis und spätantiker Geist* (Göttingen: Vandenhoeck & Ruprecht, 1954); Hans Jonas, "Gnosticism and Modern Nihilism," *Social Research* 19 (1952): 430–52. To the *Corpus Hermeticum,* the witness to the crisis, see André M. J. Festugière, *La Révélation de l'Hermes Trismégiste* (Paris, 1944–54), vol. 4.

10. E.g., Hal Koch, *Pronoia und Paideusis* (Berlin: de Gruyter, 1932), pp. 180–314; Nilsson, "Die Griechen," pp. 394–417.

11. Plato *Symposium* 202A–212B.

12. Wolfhart Pannenberg, "Die Aufnahme des philosophischen Gottesbegriffs als dogmatisches Problem der frühchristlichen Theologie," *ZKG* 70 (1959): 1–45; Yehoshua Amir, "Die Begegnung des

biblischen und des philosophischen Monotheismus," *EvTh* 38 (1978): 2–19.

13. Theophilus of Antioch *Apology to Autolycus* 1.2.5. See also Melito of Sardis *Address to Antonius Caesar* 6–8; Tatian *Address to the Greeks* 4; Justin Martyr *Dialogue with Trypho* 3.

14. If they did not content themselves altogether with the concepts of Hellenic popular theosophy, as did the earliest apology preserved; see *The Apology of Aristides on Behalf of the Christians*, ed. J. Rendel Harris, 2d ed., TaS 1/1 (Cambridge, Eng.: University Press, 1893).

15. Ignatius *Letter to the Ephesians* 7.2. See Jaroslav Pelikan, *The Emergence of the Catholic Tradition* (Chicago: University of Chicago Press, 1971), pp. 52ff.; René Braun, *"Deus Christianorum": Recherches sur le vocabulaire doctrinal de Tertullien* (Paris: Universitaire, 1962), pp. 62ff.; Werner Elert, *Der Ausgang der altchristlichen Christologie* (Berlin: Lutherisches Verlagshaus, 1957), pp. 72ff. For examples of the notion itself, Nemesius *On the Nature of Man*, in *PG* 40:673; in a pagan, Plutarch *Isis and Osiris* 54.

16. Pelikan, *Emergence*, pp. 52ff.

17. Justin Martyr *Trypho* 3.

18. Justin Martyr *Apology I* 12, 13, 25; Tatian *Greeks* 4; Melito of Sardis *Antonius Caesar* 2; Theophilus of Antioch *Autolycus* 1.3; Athenagoras *Supplication for the Christians* 10. To Justin's theology, L. W. Bernard, *Justin Martyr, His Life and Thought* (Cambridge, Eng.: University Press, 1967), pp. 79ff.

19. Justin Martyr *Apology II* 12. See Bernard, *Justin Martyr*, pp. 77–78; Braun, *Deus*, p. 74.

20. Justin Martyr *Trypho* 108.

21. Justin Martyr *Apology I* 19.

22. Ibid., 12.

23. Ibid., 28.

24. Justin Martyr *Trypho* 1.

25. Ibid., 11.

26. The main section of Theophilus' *Apology to Autolycus* (1.4ff.), a heaping up of adjectives in praise of God, is an especially clear example of indiscrimination. On the failure of creative synthesis, Pannenberg, "Aufnahme," pp. 312–46.

27. Ignatius *Letter to the Ephesians* 7.2; *Letter to Polycarp* 3.2.

28. Melito of Sardis provides the most startling early examples of both. See *Antonius Caesar*, frag. 13: "The Invisible is seen . . . , the

Ungraspable is laid hold of . . . , the Boundless is bounded . . . , the Impassible suffers . . . , the Deathless dies . . ."; frag. 14: ". . . walking the earth and filling heaven . . . , as man in want and as God nourishing the world . . . , he stood before Pilate and was sitting by his Father; he was fixed to the cross and was upholding the universe"; in frag. 16 he delivers both jolts at once: "God was killed."

29. E.g., Gregory Nazianzus *Orations* 27, 32, 38, 29.19–20.

30. "God" as a predicate of Jesus is entirely unproblematic in the paradox christology. Melito of Sardis already has the full formula to be later so painfully recovered; *Antonius Caesar*, frag. 6: "at once God and perfect man."

31. Pelikan, *Emergence*, pp. 136–82; F. H. Kettler, "Trinität: Dogmengeschichtlich," *RGG*³ 3:1026ff.

32. According to Tertullian *Against Praxeas* 3.1, opining that modalism is the favorite of "the simple . . . , who are always a majority of the faithful."

33. The first great antimodalist work was Tertullian's *Against Praxeas*, ca. 207 A.D. In principle, another has never been needed.

34. Thus in Lactantius we have a purely mythological trinitarianism and christology. The Son is an almost-God who covers himself with flesh to teach those in the flesh. The conceptual framework is provided by hermeticism. See Aloys Grillmeier, *Christ in Christian Tradition*, trans. J. S. Bowden (New York: Sheed & Ward, 1965), 1:190–206. Also the Apologists' theology is in fact mythological, as is plain in Justin, whose doctrine is of a second God, with all the actual divine work to do. How completely Justin thought of a middle realm of mythic partial divinities is shown in *Apology I* 6.

35. See Hermann Kleinknecht, "Logos," *ThWNT* 4:71–89.

36. E.g., the *Theologia Graeca* 16: "Hermes is the Logos, whom the gods sent us from heaven, to make man rational *(logikos)* . . . , but even more to save us. . . . He is sent as . . . messenger of the gods, to teach men of them."

37. Justin Martyr *Apology I* 32.

38. Justin Martyr *Trypho* 127. Theophilus of Antioch has the same argument in *Autolycus* 2.22.

39. Justin Martyr *Trypho* 10.126–28; 13; *Apology I* 62–63.

40. Justin Martyr *Dialogue* 55–62.

41. Justin Martyr *Apology II* 6, 13.

42. Athenagoras *Supplication* 10; Theophilus of Antioch *Autolycus* 2.10. Cf. *Epistle to Diognetus* 8.9–9.1 (stated with a social analogy).

43. Theophilus of Antioch *Autolycus* 22; Athenagoras *Supplication* 10; Justin Martyr *Trypho* 61.

44. E.g., Justin Martyr *Apology I* 5. Justin Martyr uses the Logos concept also apologetically, to relate the truth in Christ to truth known apart from him. The Logos is the "Sower" of reason in all reality; thus all knowledge is the result of the "seeds of the Logos"; in Christ, the Sower himself is present among us (see *Apology II* 8, 10, 12, 13). But the apologetic problem is not really a separate problem from that of distance between God and time, for over against God's absence, salvation must be conceived of as revelation, and then it is precisely any antecedent knowledge to which salvation must be related.

45. See Braun, *Deus*, pp. 289–91; Justin Martyr *Trypho* 62, 128.

46. See Georg Kretschmar, *Studien zur früchristlichen Trinitätstheologie* (Tübingen: J. C. B. Mohr, 1956), pp. 1–15.

47. And both in fact appeared in this period. Lactantius was a crude binitarian; Eusebius of Caesarea, for example, was a sophisticated one. In Athenagoras *Supplication* 10, we have a "multitude" of mediators.

48. See Tatian *Greeks* 7; Theophilus of Antioch (*Autolycus* 2.15), on the other hand, follows a Jewish tradition in which the biblical "Sophia" passages are interpreted of the one of God's "two hands," while the Logos is the other. See Kretschmar, *Studien*, pp. 40–61. Theophilus calls also the Logos "Wisdom"; *Autolycus* 2.10. This will not be sorted out for centuries; see Pelikan, *Emergence*, pp. 185–86.

49. So Justin Martyr *Apology I* 13.

50. See the introduction by J. Armitage Robinson, ed., in *Irenaeus: The Demonstration of the Apostolic Preaching* (London: SPCK, 1920).

51. Athenagoras *Supplication* 15–22.

52. In the very style of Karl Barth's *Commentary on Romans*.

53. *Epistle to Diognetus* 7.2; 8.7–9.1.

54. Though the biblical language dominates; e.g., Irenaeus *Against All Heresies* 2.2.4; 2.10.1; 2.30.9. See also Robinson, ed., *Irenaeus*, pp. 6–23.

55. Irenaeus *Heresies* 2.1–2; 2.6.

56. Ibid., 2.7.6; 2.8.2; 2.13.4–6, 8.

57. Ibid., 2.2.5.

58. Ibid., 4.2.1.

59. Ibid., 2.28.6; see Gustav Wingren, *Man and the Incarnation* (Philadelphia: [Muhlenberg] Fortress Press, 1959), p. 4.

60. Irenaeus *Heresies* 2.28.6.

61. E.g., ibid., 4.20.3.

62. E.g., ibid., 3.9.2–3; 2.6.1; 3.12.13.

63. Ibid., 2.4.3.

64. Wingren, *Man,* pp. 81ff.

65. E.g., Irenaeus *Demonstration* 6, 47–50; *Heresies* 1.10.1.

66. Irenaeus *Demonstration* 47.

67. Irenaeus *Heresies* 3.22.3.

68. The developments in Christianity and paganism, at least in the East, were parallel. In paganism, from Middle Platonism to Plotinus; in Christianity, from the Apologists to Origen.

69. E.g., Tertullian *Praxeas* 2.1–2.

70. Pelikan, *Emergence,* pp. 104–5, 179–80.

71. Braun, *Deus,* pp. 38, 77–78.

72. Ibid., pp. 52–56.

73. Ibid., pp. 34–35.

74. Tertullian *On the Flesh of Christ* 5.1.

75. Ibid., 5.3–4.

76. Ibid., 3.5.

77. Tertullian *Praxeas* 5.1–6; Braun, *Deus,* pp. 256–70.

78. Tertullian *Praxeas* 7.1.

79. Braun, *Deus,* pp. 250–62, 270; Pelikan, *Emergence,* p. 187.

80. Tertullian *Praxeas* 3.5; 8.7; 9.2.

81. Ibid., 5.1.

82. Ibid., 16.4. See also 14–15; 16.2–3; 19.6.

83. Ibid., 8.7.

84. Ibid., 3.2–5.

85. Braun, *Deus,* pp. 158–67.

86. Tertullian *Praxeas* 2.4.

87. Braun, pp. 107–9.

88. Both of the Latin and of the Greek equivalent, *prosopon.*

89. Braun, *Deus,* pp. 212–16. E.g., Irenaeus *Demonstration* 49; Justin Martyr *Apology I* 36; Theophilus of Antioch *Autolycus* 2.22; Tertullian himself, *Praxeas* 9.3.

90. Braun, *Deus,* pp. 216–32.

91. Ibid., pp. 228–32. Since the point is that the role distinctions of the Son and the Spirit from the Father are real, Tertullian first argues for the substantiality of the Son and the Spirit, then introduces *persona* for the particular sort of reality wanted; *Praxeas* 7.9; 12.9.

92. E.g., *Praxeas* 21ff.

93. Ibid., 11.9–10. See Braun, *Deus*, p. 235: "A *person*, that is, is first and foremost someone who speaks and acts. The Son converses with the Father, that is the scriptural given."

94. Tertullian *Praxeas* 7.9; 4.4.

95. Ibid., 12.3.

96. Braun, *Deus*, pp. 142–50.

97. Ibid., p. 150.

98. It was introduced by Seneca as a translation of the Stoics' *hypostasis*, was used also to translate their *hypokeimenon*, and by Tertullian's time was the accepted translation of *ousia*. See ibid., pp. 173–94.

99. Braun, *Deus*, pp. 150, 188ff.

100. Tertullian *Praxeas* 8.4.

101. The recasting of Tertullian's trinitarianism in proper Aristotelian-Platonist categories was already completed by Novatian ca. A.D. 250; Novatian *On the Trinity*, e.g., 2.12; 5.6.

102. E.g., Origen *On First Principles* 1.1.5–6; see Robert W. Jenson, *The Knowledge of Things Hoped For* (New York: Oxford University Press, 1969), pp. 26ff.

103. Origen *First Principles* 1.1.8.

104. It is the bondage of our mind to time that separates us from God; Origen *Commentary on John*, frags. 1, 13.

105. Origen *First Principles* 1.1.6; 4.3.15; 4.2.7; see Jenson, *Knowledge*, pp. 37ff.

106. Origen *On First Principles* 2.6.1.

107. Hans Willms, *EIKŌN* (Münster: Aschendorff, 1938), pp. 1–24; Jenson, *Knowledge*, pp. 34–36.

108. Plato *Timaeus* 28A–29C; 48E–49A.

109. Willms, *EIKŌN*, pp. 25ff.; Henri Crouzel, *Théologie de l'image de Dieu chez Origène* (Paris: Aubier, 1951), pp. 25ff.; Werner Jaeger, *Nemesius von Emessa* (Berlin: Weidmann, 1914); Jenson, *Knowledge*, pp. 36–37.

110. Jenson, *Knowledge*, pp. 25ff.

111. Origen *John* 1.17.

112. Ibid., 22.29. See also *Against Celsus* 8.12; *First Principles* 1.2.6.

113. Origen *John* 2.2.

114. Origen *First Principles* 2.6.3.

115. Ibid., 1.2.2.

116. Ibid.

117. Ibid., 1.2.3.

118. Ibid., 1.2.5; 1.2.2; 1.2.9; 4.4.1.

119. Origen *John,* frag. 21; 1.38.

120. Ibid., 2.2.

121. Origen *First Principles* 1.3.4.

122. Ibid., 1.3.8; 2.7.2. Cf. Kretschmar, *Studien,* pp. 7–8.

123. Origen *First Principles* 1.3.5, 8.

124. Ibid., 1.3.8; 1.6.2.

125. Ibid., 1.3.4.

126. Ibid., 1.3.4; 4.3.14; Origen *Commentary on Isaiah* 1.2; *Commentary on Ezekiel* 14.2. See Kretschmar, *Studien,* pp. 64–68.

127. Origen *First Principles* 1.4.3.

128. Ibid., 1.8.3; 4.4.1.

129. Ibid., 4.4.6.

130. Ibid., 3.5.13.

131. Ibid., 3.5.10; 1.4.3; 2.4.3; 3.5.4.

132. Ibid., 3.3.3.

133. Ibid., 2.4.3. Whether the place in which Origen directly calls the Son a "creature" (4.4.1) is authentic is disputed.

134. Ibid., 1.3.5. Origen evidently did not notice or want to notice another possibility within his own trinitarian solution, which would have broken through subordinationism: ranking Son and Spirit alongside each other as images of God rather than in series. The greatest of his immediate pupils did notice it but had little influence; Gregory Thaumaturgos *To Philagrius* 5.

135. Origen *First Principles* 4.2.7; 4.3.14.

136. Origen *John* 2.3.

137. On the general development after Origen, see Friedrich Loofs, *Leitfaden zum Studium der Dogmengeschichte,* 5th ed., ed. Kurt Aland (Halle: Niemeyer, 1951), 1:169–82.

138. Eusebius of Caesarea *Demonstration of the Gospel* 4.1.

139. Ibid.

140. Ibid., 5.4, throughout.

141. Ibid., 5.9–30.

142. Ibid., 4.5.

143. Ibid., 4.3.

144. Ibid. and 5.8.

145. Ibid., 3.15; 4.2.

146. Ibid. and 5.4.

147. Ibid., 5.11.

148. Athanasius *Against the Pagans,* e.g., 46; *Discourse on the Incarnation of the Word.*

149. Athanasius *Pagans* 2.34.

150. Athanasius *Incarnation* 54.

151. Athanasius *Pagans* 9–29.

152. Ibid., 40, 41.

153. Ibid., 47.

154. Ibid., 2, 23.

155. Athanasius *Incarnation* 11–13.

156. Ibid., 9.27.40.

157. On Lucian and the Lucianists, see Gustave Bardy, *Recherches sur Saint Lucien d'Antioch et son École* (Paris: Beauchesne, 1936). Here the remaining Lucianist texts are collected; on the rallying of the Lucianists, pp. 217ff.

158. J. N D. Kelly, *Early Christian Doctrines* (New York: Harper & Row, 1960), p. 231.

159. On the following history, see Louis Duchesne, *Early History of the Christian Church* (New York: Longmans, Green, 1912), 2:98ff.; Grillmeier, *Christ*, pp. 219ff.; Kelly, *Doctrines*, pp. 193–251.

160. Arius *Letter to Eusebius*, in Bardy, *Recherches*, p. 227; "We do not chime in with those who daily say, 'Always God, always Son. . . .'"

161. Ibid.

162. Asterius, the Lucianists' chief publicist, stated the principle; see fragments in Bardy, *Recherches*, pp. 335–57.

163. Arius *Thalia*, in Bardy, *Recherches*, p. 286.

164. Arius *Letter to Alexander*, in Bardy, *Recherches*, pp. 236–37.

165. Arius *Eusebius*, in Bardy, *Recherches*, p. 228.

166. Arius as cited by Athanasius *Discourse Against the Arians III* 27.

167. Arius *Alexander*, in Bardy, *Recherches*, p. 237.

168. Arius *Eusebius*, in Bardy, *Recherches*, p. 228.

169. E.g., Alexander *Letter to Alexander* [of Constantinople] 2.

170. Arius *Alexander*, in Bardy, *Recherches*, pp. 235–36.

171. Alexander *Alexander* 11.

172. Ibid., 5.

173. Arius *Alexander*, in Bardy, *Recherches*, p. 236.

174. Arius *Thalia*, in Bardy, *Recherches*, p. 261.

175. Arius as reported by Alexander *Letter to His Colleagues* 3.

176. Arius *Thalia*, in Bardy, *Recherches*, p. 256.

177. Ibid., frags. 12, 13.

178. Eunomius, as cited by Gregory of Nyssa *Against Eunomius* in his *Opera*, vols. 1–2, ed. W. Jaeger (Leiden: Brill, 1952), 3/8.14: "The

mind *(nous)* . . . of those who have believed in the Lord, when it has transcended all sensible and intelligible being, does not naturally stop at the origin of the Son but goes beyond even that, seeking to encounter the very first source of eternal life."

179. Initially, there were two other great polemicists. Marcellus of Ancyra dropped out because he turned out to be theologically dubious. Eustathius of Antioch was offended mostly by the Arians' specific christology, and his views belong in that locus.

180. Athanasius *Discourse III* 6.

181. Athanasius *Epistle on the Decrees of Nicaea* 2; *Discourse Against the Arians I* 12.14; *Decrees* 12.

182. E.g., Gregory of Nyssa *Eunomius* 1.382, 591–92, 628–730.

183. Athanasius *Discourse I* 14, 28; *Discourse III* 66; *Discourse I* 20; *Discourse III* 63.

184. Athanasius *Discourse III* 15. See also 16, 64; *Discourse I* 8.10.18.

185. Athanasius *Discourse III* 18. See also *Letter to Adelphius* 3.

186. Athanasius *Nicaea* 13. See *Discourse I* 29–34.

187. Athanasius *Letter to Serapion I* (PG 26:529–608), 30: "Just as baptism given in 'the Father and the Son and the Holy Spirit' is one and there is one confession of faith . . . , so the holy Trinity, identical with itself in itself and united to itself, has no creature in itself." See also *Discourse I* 34; *Discourse Against the Arians II* (PG 26:145–321), 42; *Nicaea* 31; *Serapion I* 6.

188. Athanasius *Serapion I* 29–30.

189. E.g., Basil the Great *Letters* (PG 32:219–1114), 125.3: "For the mark of right understanding [here with respect to the Spirit] is not to separate him from the Father and the Son; for we must be baptized as we have received the command, and confess as we have been baptized, and worship as we have confessed: Father and Son and Holy Spirit." Gregory of Nyssa *Eunomius* 1.314: "God the Logos himself, when he gave to the disciples the mystery [baptism] of the knowledge of God, said that the life of the reborn is fulfilled and renewed in the name 'Father, Son, and Holy Spirit.'" For the nuances of Nicene use of the baptismal invocation, see Kretschmar, *Studien*, pp. 125–34. Kretschmar does not, it should be noted, fully support my interpretation of the Athanasian passages.

190. Gregory Nazianzus *Orations* 32.28.

191. The text of the relevant part of the second article and of the appended anathemas: "And in one Lord, Jesus Christ, the Son of God; born of the Father *(ek tou patros)* uniquely, i.e., out of the being

of the Father *(ek tes ousias tou patros)*; God of God; light of light; true God of true God; born, not made; of one being *(homoousion)* with the Father. . . ." "The catholic church condemns those who say 'there was when he was not' and 'before he was born he was not' and 'he originated from what is not,' calling him either 'of another *hypostasis*' or 'of another *ousia*,' so that he would be a changeable and mutable 'Son of God.'"

192. See Athanasius *Nicaea* 19.

193. All metaphysics hinges on the doctrine of "internal relations"!

194. Athanasius *Letter to Serapion II* 6.

195. Heinz Kraft, "'OMOOUSIOS,'" *ZKG* 66 (1954–55): 1–24; Grillmeier, *Christ*, pp. 249–73; above all the splendid excursus in Adolf M. Ritter, *Das Konzil von Konstantinopel und sein Symbol* (Göttingen: Vandenhoeck & Ruprecht, 1965), pp. 270–93.

196. Origen, frag. 540, as collected in *EnchP.*

197. Arius *Thalia*, in Bardy, *Recherches*, p. 256.

198. Constantine's chief adviser was Hosius of Cordoba. On his role, see Kraft, "'OMOOUSIOS.'"

199. Cf. Grillmeier, *Christ*, 1:275–96.

200. Louis Duchesne, *Early History of the Christian Church* (New York: Longmans, Green, 1915), pp. 98ff.

201. *Ousia* was a word of many acceptations. But as the active verbal substantive of "to be," it always carried the feel of—to make a barbarism—"an is-er," that which "is-es," "reality" not as a characterization of the real over against the unreal, but as a verbal noun for the real itself. As theology became more philosophically technical through the fourth and fifth centuries, Aristotle's and Plato's more specific analyses and doctrines of being became more determinative.

202. For a sprightly telling of this melancholy tale, see Duchesne, *History*, pp. 125–200, 128ff.; for the theology, Michel Meslin, *Les Ariens des l'Occident* (Paris: Seuil, 1967), pp. 253–99.

203. On the exceptions, see Meslin, *Ariens*, pp. 29–99.

204. Urged on by Hilary of Poitiers, "the Athanasius of the West." His *On the Trinity* is a pioneering mixture of Eastern and Western theology, historically important, but not for our story.

205. Athanasius *Epistle on the Councils* 51; *Discourse III* 3.

206. Athanasius *Discourse I* 9.

207. Athanasius *Nicaea* 20.

208. Athanasius *Councils* 41–42.

209. Athanasius *Discourse III* 5.

210. Athanasius *Discourse I* 18.

211. Where *ousia* = *physis*.

212. Where *ousia* = Aristotle's "first substance."

213. See Gregory Nazianzus *Orations* 21.20.

214. Basic is Origen *Against Celsus* 8.12.

215. See Ritter, *Konzil*, pp. 64–85.

216. Duchesne, *History*, 1:276–77.

217. Ritter, *Konzil*, pp. 68–85.

218. Athanasius *Ariminum* 43.

219. Gregory of Nyssa *Refutation of Eunomius' Confession* (in his *Opera*, vol. 2), 30–40.

220. Gregory Nazianzus *Letter CI* 192B.

221. On the history, see Ritter, *Konzil*, pp. 21–40.

222. This has long been controversial, but Ritter, ibid., pp. 132–208, has in my view settled the matter.

223. On the pneumatology of Constantinople, see the excursus in ibid., pp. 293–307. There were apparently a series of clumsy post-Nicene attempts to synthesize the concerns by admitting the "*homo-ousia*" of the Son and then subordinating the Spirit to both, thus still preserving a mediating hierarchy; see Adolf Laminski, *Der Heilige Geist als Geist Christi und Geist der Gläubigen* (Leipzig: St. Benno, 1969), pp. 30–35. Already in a synod at Alexandria in 362, Athanasius—again—made recognition of the Spirit's full deity a test of church fellowship, and the spirits divided from that date; ibid., pp. 120–25. Athanasius recognized in Spirit-subordinationism the same religious principle as in Arianism, and also in this case labeled it polytheism; *Letter to Serapion I* 1–2, 10, 28–30. See Laminski, *Heilige Geist*, pp. 57–58.

224. Ritter, *Konzil*, pp. 68–85.

225. Ibid., pp. 133–51, 172–75, 204–8.

4

The One and the Three

The Cappadocian Language

Two centuries of passionate reflection brought the Eastern church back to the rule of faith with which it began. But now there is an agreed type of formula, for instance, "there is one deity in the Trinity, in the Father and in the Son, and . . . in the Holy Spirit, as in that same Trinity there is one baptism and one Creed."[1] And there is a conceptuality provided by the Cappadocians: "one *being (ousia)* of God in three *hypostases (hypostaseis)*." The conceptuality was derived from expressions of Origen,[2] and at a second session of Theodosius' council, in 382, was taken into approved ecclesiastical use.[3] In elucidating it, I will explicate the Cappadocian analysis and continue to some analysis of my own.

At a first level, "one being in three hypostases" was merely a sort of linguistic settlement, stipulating terminology for a perceived need that somehow we be able to refer separately to one and to three realities of God. In most theological use, *ousia* and *hypostasis* had been handled as rough equivalents. The decree of Nicaea used both indiscriminately in the singular in asserting the oneness of the triune reality, as did Athanasius all his life.[4] The entire Origenist spectrum used both in the plural in asserting that there really are three somehow different realities in the Trinity.[5] The new terminological regulation, finding two words for "what is real" in trinitarian use, split the difference and took one for the one and the other for the three.

Thereby the East was provided with a trinitarian terminology extensionally equivalent to the West's "one substance (*substan-*

103

tia) in three persons (*personae*)." But it is vital to understand that the two terminologies are not intensionally equivalent. If a proposition in the one is simply set into the other, its meaning is not necessarily preserved.[6] Failure to observe this has been and is the cause of a great deal of confusion. "Substance" and "person" had never been interchangeable. Just so, their distinction evoked no new insight, nor did they carry any history of trinitarian controversy.[7]

Ousia and *hypostasis* both came into theology from the philosophical tradition,[8] where they were used almost interchangeably for *what is*—conformably to Hellenic apprehension, for what is by possession of some specific complex of permanent characteristics. Just so, they were also used for the "being" so possessed.

In further conformity to Hellenic apprehension, these reality-giving characteristics then also functioned as identifying characteristics, to mark each reality out from what surrounds it.[9] Identification proceeds pyramid-fashion. Socrates, for instance, is identified by certain characteristics as a living being among natural entities, by other characteristics as an animal among living beings, and by yet others as a human among animals. Here there is a break, for with Socrates identified simply as Socrates, over against, say, Cratylus and Meno, we arrive at individuality and so at contingency and unpredictability, that is, as the Greeks interpreted reality, at the edge of nonbeing. What Socrates *is* is *a human*. The individually identifying characteristics that differentiate him from other humans are therefore in themselves manifestations of imperfection, of ways in which different individuals can fall short of the ideal humanity.[10]

Between *ousia* and *hypostasis* there were, nevertheless, slight nuances of difference. *Ousia* tended to be used for the reality that real things have and so to evoke, for example, the humanity that Socrates has, but not so much the marks by which he as a human differs from other beings, while *hypostasis* sounded most strongly the notes of distinguishability and identifiability. When trinitarian use divided the terms, the division was made along the line of these nuances. *Hypostasis* now meant simply that which can be identified, while *ousia* meant *what* such an identifiable *is*. This necessarily dropped *hypostasis* to the level of individuals, and located *ousia* as the word for the kind of being any one kind of individuals have in common[10]—except that *hypostasis* brought with it an aura of metaphysical dignity that previous terms lacked.

Just this is the starting position of the Cappadocian analysis: Father, Son, and Spirit, they say, are three individuals who share Godhead, as Peter, Paul, and Barnabas are three individuals who share humanity.[12] The one being of God is common to the three hypostases, which are distinguished by individually identifying characteristics of "being unbegotten," "being begotten," and "proceeding."[13] Clearly this lays them open to this question: "As Peter, Paul, and Barnabas are three men, why are Father, Son, and Spirit not three gods?"[14] The Cappadocians' metaphysical creativity appears in their answer to this challenge.

Hypostasis / Identity

The Cappadocians reworked the concepts *ousia* and *hypostasis*. We will consider *hypostasis* first. The plural individuals that share humanity differ from one another by characteristics adventitious to—indeed, in the usual Hellenic view, privative of—the humanity they have in common, by brown hair, moderate intelligence, Athenian ancestry, or whatever. Just so, they are plural humans. But, said the Cappadocians, Godhead can receive no such adventitious or privative characteristics. Therefore there is no way for a plurality of divine hypostases, if their plurality is somehow established, to make a plurality of Gods.[15] Their argument, it should be noted, holds only if the graded adjectival use of "God" has become utterly inconceivable, which is just what Christian theological self-consciousness had by now achieved.

And, according to the Cappadocians, there is indeed a way, without characteristics adventitious to or privative of Godhead, for the three to be individually identified. Their individually identifying characteristics are the relations they have to each other, precisely with respect to their joint possession of deity.[16] God is the Father as the source of the Son's and the Spirit's Godhead; God is the Son as the recipient of the Father's Godhead; and God is the Spirit as the spirit of the Son's possession of the Father's Godhead.[17] The different ways in which each is the *one* God, for and from the others, are the only differences between them.[18] We have arrived at a certain completion of the dialectic. Since all the hypostases are is distinguishable something in God, and since they are distinguished only by their relations to each other, there is only one step remaining—not however explicitly taken until centuries later—and that is to say that the hypostases simply *are* "relations subsisting in God."[19] These formulations have since remained unchanged in the tradition.

We have also arrived at a point where more than historical interpretation and reflection is needed. There are two matters to consider. First, we must remind ourselves what all these word games are about. The "hypostases" are Jesus and the transcendent Will he called "Father" and the Spirit of their future for us. Just as vital to remember, the hypostases' "relations" are Jesus' historical obedience to and dependence on his "Father" and the coming of their Spirit into the believing community. "Begetting," "being begotten," "proceeding," and their variants are biblical terms for temporal structures of evangelical history, which theology then uses for relations said to be constitutive of God's life.[20] What happens between Jesus and his Father and our future *happens in God*—that is the point.

It was the achievement of the Cappadocians to find a conceptualized way to say this, by arranging Origen's hypostases and their *homoousia* horizontally[21] to time rather than vertically to time, making the hypostases' mutual relations structures of the one God's life rather than risers of the steps from God down to us.[22] The Trinity as such is now understood to be the Creator, over against the creature, and the three in God and their relations become the evangelical history's reality on the Creator-side of the great biblical Creator/creature divide.

Across the Creator/creature distinction, no mediator is needed.[23] "Creator"/"creature" names an absolute difference but no *distance* at all, for to be the Creator is merely as such to be actively related to the creature. Each of the inner-trinitarian relations is then an affirmation that as God works creatively among us, so he is in himself.

The proposition that the relations are themselves what subsist in God as the possessors of Godhead is initially a solution for a purely dialectical problem. But if the trinitarian analysis is on the right track, a solution to one of its internal problems should be translatable into soteriology. And so this one can be: It is just and only in that "the Father" *gives,* Jesus obediently *receives,* and their Future *is sent to* us that the relation of Creator to creature is established in the evangelical events, that these three are, so to speak, on both sides of the God/creature line. It is by the temporal dynamic between Jesus and his Father and our Destiny, that the three are *God.*

Perhaps we can show something of what is being said by analyzing once more the Christian address to God as "Father." Use of this word is neither a mere analogy, in principle replaceable by some other, nor yet, of course, a univocal description, as if God were sexually responsible for our existence. In historical fact, Jesus addressed God filially; as we have seen, there was—and is—no word but "Father" by which to fulfill this address. And it is precisely this filial *relation* between Jesus and the One on whom he depended, by which there *is* the God we worship. The "analogy" by which we call God "Father" is therefore not merely our linguistic device; the historical occurrence of this analogical communication between Jesus and Transcendence is *constitutive* for God himself.[24] By the exact whole structure just described, the reality of God allows and commands people to address him with the Father-metaphor and—within its range—none other. And in that our communication with God is thus controlled by his reality, it is true.

It is time, I said, to remind ourselves of these things. The Nicene dogma and the Cappadocian analysis were victories in

the confrontation between the gospel's and Hellenism's interpretations of God. But the confrontation is by no means con-
cluded, and one continuous post-Nicene threat has been the
temptation to interpret the Trinity-as-a-whole by the negative
theology, so that the Trinity in its turn disappears into the old
distant timelessness, carrying its internal reflection of evangelical history right with it. Already in the Cappadocians there
is a danger signal: their tendency to take refuge in mystery
when asked what "begetting" and "proceeding" *mean.*[25] Why
should there be a problem? There is none about what these
words mean as slogans for saving historical events. No more
should there be about their trinitarian meanings—unless the
understanding of the triune life itself is infiltrated with impassibility, immobility, and so on, with reference to which a word
like "proceeding" indeed cannot mean much.

The temporal reference of trinitarian language reaffirmed,
we can turn again to the conceptual problem of the three hypostases. The separation of *hypostasis* from *ousia* was a creative
disruption of Hellenic interpretation of reality, by which disruption the triune God's peculiar reality became speakable. But
hypostasis opens the new vision only by way of this event in its
history, and not by way of its ordinary ancient or modern uses.
As a piece of trinitarian language, *hypostasis* is merely an item
of linguistic debris knocked from Hellenic philosophy by col-
lision with Yahweh. Present understanding would be ad-
vanced if we replaced it with a word now philosophically active; readers will not be surprised that I propose "identity,"
for as is apparent from the history of the adaptation of *hypostasis* to trinitarian use, it is exactly the ontological function now
marked by "identity" that the trinitarian *hypostasis*, in its separation from *ousia*, invoked. I explicate this function in three
steps.

First, something's identity is the possibility of picking it out
from the maelstrom of actuality, so as to talk about it. The
enumerability of the world, whereby we can say "this, and
this, and then this," is one of the world's deepest metaphysical
characters. This character, taken of any one such "this," is an
identity.

We identify in various ways. We point and say "this." But often we cannot point. Then we have two linguistic resources: proper names and identifying descriptions, as was discussed earlier.

Accordingly, that there are three identities in God means that there are three discrete sets of names and descriptions, each sufficient to specify uniquely, yet all identifying the same reality. Among them that which says, "God is what happens with Jesus," has the epistemological priority of the present tense, so that in each of the other two, terms will appear which, if interpretation is required, can only be interpreted by reference to Jesus' story. For example, if we say, "God is the Hope at the beginning of all things," and are asked, "Hope for what?" we must answer, "Hope for Jesus' triumph."

The three identifications can otherwise be performed independently. But the *predicates* we use of the one identified in any of the three ways can be made unambiguous—should ambiguity threaten—only by running them across all three identities. For example, "God is good in the way that a giver is good, and he is good in the way that a gift is good, and he is good in the way that the outcome of a gift is good."

Second, to identify something is to pick it out *as* something *otherwise* known. Only that has identity which is repeatedly identifiable. I am identical with myself in that I am identifiable *as* the one I was before or will be later: "I am the one who called yesterday—remember?" In such a sequence as "It was brown, and it is green, and I suppose it may be purple next," the identity—*hypostasis*—is the possibility of the repeated "it."

In the metaphysical tradition stemming from Greece, the usual understanding is that the possibility of repeated identification lies in the prolongation of some one identification. Insofar as a thing is real, according to this doctrine, there is a complex of characters which it possesses timelessly, which it must continue to exemplify so long as it is anything at all. An identifying description drawn from these characters will always, therefore, work. The first point of "three identities" is that with God, at least, there is no such one identity. Yet the three, it is asserted, are *of* one reality, and their plurality, moreover, has a structure of tenses. The reality of God is repeatedly identified, and so has identity, without being defined by any one timelessly exemplified set of characteristics.

We should note immediately how radical a revision this is of the concept of deity. The very point about God had been that in distinction from all other being all his characters are essential, so that his self-identity encompasses them all and is therefore immune to all determination from outside itself—so that he is impassible. We remain ourselves so long as we remain at all—but that may not be very long. God remains so long as he is himself—which, given that he ever is, must thus be forever. Since this particular sort of eternity rests on the universality of this God's self-identity, it encompasses an incapability for any change whatever; this God is *changeless*. The assertion of the three identities discards all this; what it is replaced by, we will see later.

Third, "identity" is now regularly used to interpret personal existence, as we may say that someone is "seeking his identity." This sense is connected to the other two; it names the mode of repeated identifiability proper to certain entities, those we currently call "personal" in a sense—note well—very different from the trinitarian "person." As person, in this modern sense, I am what I am only in that I remember what I have been and hope for what I will be. If Jones is a person, in this modern sense, the "is" in "Jones is lazy," for instance, is not quite a normal copula; it is more like a transitive verb modifiable by adverbs. We might better say, "Jones ises Jones, lazily." "Is" is here the word for a specific *act* of positing oneself in and through time. Existentialist thought has invented words like "existence" or *"Dasein"* for this act.

Hypostasis in its pretrinitarian and prechristological uses did not have this sense. But in the often tortured ways in which the theological tradition has used *hypostasis,* just this sense for the peculiar identity of person-realities struggled for expression already in the Cappadocians.

Accordingly, that there is even one identity of God means that God is personal, that he *is* God in that he *does* Godhead, in that he chooses himself as God. That there are three identities in God means that this God's deed of being the one God is three times repeated, and so that each repetition is a being of God, and so that only in this precise self-repetition is God the particular God that he in fact is. God does God, and over again, and yet over again—and only so does the event and decision that is this God occur.

"Being" or "Event"

Back to the Cappadocians. Beside a word for the three, they needed also a correlated analysis of the one divine *ousia* to show how it *could* be the being of three individuals without these being three instances of God. They had a variety of arguments, all involving a key assertion that the Christian God is infinite. Because Gregory of Nyssa was the most powerful analyst of this point, and because we will continue with his thought in the next chapter, we will here follow one of his arguments.

Since there is only one Godhead, the Trinity is a kind of individual and must therefore be identifiable if real—despite the claim that God allows of no one identification. And Gregory indeed provides an identifying description of the one *ousia* of God—but this is precisely that God's being is infinite.[26] We can identify God's one being as and only as the life that knows no boundary and that therefore will always go on to surpass each—even true—identifying description.[27] This need not mean we cannot at all identify God affirmatively; he is "the one who raised Jesus." But then we are with the three rather than the one.

Just so, conversely, it is at this level of identifying descriptions that Gregory locates—or to which he demotes—all the traditional metaphysical attributes of God in that he treats them as derivatives of infinity.[28] "Omniscient," "omnipotent," and so on, thus do no more than mark off God in the same way that "married to Xanthippe" marks off Socrates.[29] Such attributes do not mark off God from other real or possible Gods, since all Gods would be equally omniscient or whatever. Nor do they mark off deity from creaturehood, since deity, as boundless, cannot be marked off at all. They mark off the *individual*, God, from individuals of whatever sorts, just as "married to Xanthippe" does indeed mark off Socrates from a particular lamp post or a particular amoeba—however odd the notion of doing it this way in the case of Socrates. Nor are the negative attributes in any better case. Generally the Cappadocians deny any functional difference between affirmative and negative predicates of God;[30] therewith, Arianism and all its variants are taken off their logical hinges.[31]

There is also, according to Gregory, a proper name to identify the one Godhead, but it is precisely the trinitarian compound of *three* names. Following a particularly subtle analysis of the dogmatic function of the trinitarian baptismal naming, he asks why the Lord, having commanded baptism "into the name [singular]," gives not one name but three.[32] The reason, he says, is that there is no name for the being of God as one. Rather, the Lord permits us to use the names of the three together, in place of a name for the one.[33]

In consequence of these restrictions, what is for Hellenic apprehension the ontologically chief step in the identification of any real thing cannot be performed with God. By some of, for example, Socrates' characteristics, he can be marked off from being in general as a human; just so the chief truth about him is stated. There is no way to mark off God as "a God"; that is, there is no list of characteristics differentiating gods from other beings, which God must always exemplify in order to be God.

Gregory is fully aware of the break he is making with philosophical tradition. He states the view "of the many," which he rejects. According to it, "God" is, like "human" or "rock," "an unmetaphorical name by nature," predicated to identify by the nature of the thing.[34] Such a word evokes some entity's entire set of essential characters all at once, insofar as these make an organic complex so that each character is itself only together with the others. Just so, such a word uniquely displays "the underlying individual subject,"[35] that which in any real thing *has* all the characters by which that thing is what it is, and is itself established as the possible possessor of these characters and no others. For God, says Gregory, there is no such word.[36]

Thus—and we are finally to the point—Gregory's answer to the question, why three individuals sharing God's *ousia* do not make three gods, is that "God" and all its equivalents are not predicated of the divine *ousia* at all, singly or trebly. "God" is a predicate, and how many gods are asserted depends on how many logical subjects it is attached to. A plurality of instances of the divine *ousia* is not a plurality of *gods*, for the *ousia* is not the logical subject of "God" to begin with, and neither then are the *ousia*'s instances logical subjects of "God."

What then *is* "God" predicated of? Gregory's revolutionary answer is: of the divine *activity* toward us.[37] We can only say what happens to us, in that there is God. And since all divine action is the structuredly mutual work of Father, Son, and Spirit, the divine activity is but one logical subject of "God": "All action which comes upon the creature from God . . . begins from the Father and is present through the Son and is perfected in the Holy Spirit. Therefore the name of the action [God] is not divided among the plurality of the actors."[38] Gregory of Nazianzus once revised an old trinitarian illustration in an astonishing way. Instead of comparing Father, Son, and Spirit to the sun and its beams, he compared them to three suns, so focused as to make but one beam: the *beam* is God.[39]

The divine *ousia* does not drop out of the picture (we will return to it in the next chapter), for the inner-trinitarian relations, by which there are three to begin with, are defined in terms of it; it is precisely deity which the Father gives, the Son receives, and the Spirit communicates. Until the relation between the oneness of this "divine being" and the oneness of "God" as act is cleared up, we cannot fully understand or judge the Cappadocian system. But remaining for the moment at a less speculative and more liturgical and proclamatory level, the tendency of the Cappadocian analysis is clear. The divine *ousia* is no longer our first concern. It is the *work*, the creative event done as Jesus' life, death, resurrection, and future advent, done by the Father through the Son for their Spirit, that is the one God.

Surely this tendency is biblically right, at least by that understanding of the biblical witness sketched above. Stipulating an *event* as the subject of "God" imposes a task of ontological revision to which we must eventually turn, as did Gregory. But leaving that for the moment, and recalling the discussion of "identity," we obtain the following formula: There is one event, God, of three identities. Therewith my proposed basic trinitarian analysis.

The Western Version

The struggle and creation we have narrated in this and the previous chapter all took place in the Eastern church. Its results were assimilated into the West from the late fourth century on; the circumstances of the assimilation have been decisive for the thought and life of the Western church. Without attempting to judge relative importance, we may mention four such circumstances.

First, the doctrine of the Trinity came to the West as a finished product. Already for Augustine, it is simply a received fact of the church's teaching that "all who . . . wrote before me on the Trinity . . . taught that 'Father, Son, and Holy Spirit' names a divine unity of one substance in inseparable equality, so that there are not three Gods but one—although the Father begets the Son, so that the Son is not who the Father is. . . . This is my faith because it is the catholic faith."[40]

Second, in conducting trinitarian analysis and speculation in Latin, the Greek results were pressed into a terminology previously established in the Latin tradition: There is one "substance" of God (= "essence" = "nature"), in three "persons." But these terms had been through none of the Eastern conceptual wars, and when it came to the creative thrusts of such Easterners as Gregory of Nyssa, Western readers invariably missed the point. Augustine himself confessed incomprehension of the key Greek distinction: "I do not grasp what difference they intend between *ousia* and *hypostasis*."[41]

The trinitarian glossary of Western theology was provided by the writings of Boethius.[42] His classical scholarship was admirable and his presentation of trinitarian dogma correct, but his incomprehension of the Greek *theologians'* point was total. Boethius equated *physis* and *ousia,* and translated the first with *natura* and the second with *essentia.* The usual Latin for *ousia* had been *substantia.* Boethius, inventing confusions even where they could have been avoided, followed the etymologies only and used *substantia* instead for *hypostasis. Hypostasis/substantia* he then defined as naming the concrete individual thing which *has* an *ousia*—Aristotle's "first *ousia*"—thus merely reporting the philosophical use and missing the actual new use of the Greek theologians. He equated *persona* with *prosopon* and used these for a *sub*class of hypostases/substances, those that are rational, thus following no other lead than Latin everyday use. He noted that the Greek theologians did not in fact use *hypostasis* for the same range as Latins used *substantia* nor yet speak of hypostases that are not *persona,* but could see no reason why. And he even noted that his stipulated definitions should lead to asserting *three* substances in God, rather than Tertullian's one substance, "except that the church's manner of speaking excludes three substances in God"(!). Meanwhile, also *physis/ousia/natura/essentia* have been narrowed to the only one of their senses that the Greek theologians did not use in this context: the abstractable characteristics of a substance. Caught between such definitions and the inherited propositions they were supposed to elucidate, early medieval trinitarian reflection was a mere struggle for linguistic survival. Even high scholasticism never regained the insight packed into the Greek terminology. Thus Thomas Aquinas' trinitarian glossary still reproduces Boethius, although cleaning up the worst equivocations.[43]

Third, Western reception of trinitarian reflection coincided with the collapse of paganism. Thus its *function,* to identify the gospel's God over against other claimants, was not enforced by daily need.

Fourth, the work of synthesis between Eastern thought and

Western language and need was almost entirely the work of one man, Augustine, one of history's few history-shaping geniuses. His personal spiritual and intellectual experience impressed themselves on Western theology in a way unparalleled in Christian history. In much of theology, this has been a blessing, but it has blighted our trinitarianism, for Augustine experienced the triune character of God himself as one thing and the history of salvation as quite another. Thus the trinitarian formulas lost their original function.

As is well known, Augustine's way to faith had two great turnings. The first, mediated by Platonic studies, was a typical Hellenic religious turn inward and upward to the Ground of the soul: "And so, admonished to return into myself, I entered my inwardness . . . ; and I saw with a kind of eye of my soul, above that eye and above my mind,[44] a changeless Light."[45] In that light he discerned the late-Platonist divine hierarchy of One, Mind and Spirit, and thought to recognize therein also the three of churchly teaching.[46] He baptized the three "Eternity," "Truth," and "Love." The experience *of* Eternity *in* Truth *by* Love, here realized prior to and apart from knowledge of the Incarnation or the gift of the Spirit, remained in various formulations the substance of his trinitarianism. Nothing need have followed this purely Platonic experience had it not proved fleeting and by itself destructive: "And you shook my feeble gaze, shining vehemently into me. I trembled with love and horror, and found how far from you I was, in a place of utter unlikeness."[47] Only then, by this rejection, was Augustine brought to a second turn, to the Incarnate Christ, to be purified by earthly discipleship and so made capable of the divine vision: "So I sought a way to get strength sufficient to enjoy you, and did not find it until I grasped . . . the man Christ Jesus."[48] Thus knowledge of the Trinity is the inner vision of eternal truth (*intellectus!*) described by philosophy and church doctrine and in principle available apart from faith in Christ; knowledge of the saving events in Christ is temporal discipleship (*fides*) to prepare for the vision.[49] The two sorts of knowledge are of altogether different kinds.[50]

These four circumstances promoted in the West a sort of reversion to pre-Nicene thinking. Hellenic interpretation of God had never been fully overcome in the general theology of the Eastern fathers.[51] It had been overcome only by and within the trinitarian dogma and analyses themselves, and there by subtle and easily lost distinctions. The Logos christology merely as such must, after all, have a tendency to establish the triune relations in themselves as mere metaphysical realities, independent of the events of salvation; since what the Logos christology set out to mediate was a metaphysical division, the mediating occurs in a metaphysical realm. The way thus remained open for Western theology to repristinate the Apologists' old additive tactic in a new form. And that is what happened over the long history of Western theology.

The inheritance of Hellenic interpretation was received as what the scholastics would come to call "natural" theology, a supposed body of truth about God shared with the heathen and so taken to be resultant, at least in principle, from the merely created circumstances of life and the merely created religious and intellectual capacities of the soul. Such of the biblical discourse about God as was clearly not shared by the heathen was therefore thought not to be thus generally available; it was received as a higher "supernatural" body of truth about God, given only by "revelation." But when the matter is put so, the "natural" knowledge of God becomes the foundation of the "supernatural"; Homer and Plato write the first chapter in the locus on God. And so the supposed timelessness and impassibility of God inevitably determine all that follows, including the trinitarian discourse.[52]

Augustine laid down this axiomatic status of divine timelessness for all subsequent Western theology. His starting point in theology was unabashedly "natural": "What happens in your heart, when you hear the word 'God'?" And his answer was pure Platonism: "You think a greatest and highest substance, that transcends all changeable creatures. . . . And so if I ask, 'Is God changeable or unchangeable?' you will quickly respond . . . , 'God is changeless.'"[53] There is a simple distinction between creatures and God: "Speak of the changes of things, and you find 'was' and 'will be'; think God, and you find 'is' where 'was' and 'will be' cannot enter."[54] God not only does not change, he cannot; just so, "he is rightly said *to be*."[55] It is the foundation of all subsequent Western theological metaphysics, laid by Augustine, that God is "he who is,"[56] that he is "Being itself."[57]

For our purposes, the most immediately destructive consequence of this doctrine is the assertion that God is "simple," in a rigid sense that comes very close to the Arian refusal of all differentiation in God. Since it is by having "accidents," that is, characteristics that can come and go, that ordinary substances give hostages to time, God has none such.[58] As Aquinas argued it, accidents are the mark of potentiality, of capacity for otherness; this is totally absent from God.[59] But so long as there is a real difference between the substance and its characteristics, it must be possible for the substance to remain while at least some characteristics come and go, that is, some must be accidents.[60] Therefore in God there is no such difference: "God is not great by a greatness other than himself . . . ; he is great by that greatness by which he himself is that very greatness . . . ; for with God, to be and to be great are the same. . . . And similarly for goodness and eternity . . . [etc.]." In a formula: "God is called 'simple' because he *is* what he *has*."[61]

But this metaphysical axiom of Western doctrine is incompatible with the heart of Nicene trinitarianism. If all attributes of God *are* his one substance, none can be predicated of one of the identities in any special sense without "confusing" the substance and the identities. Augustine: "This Trinity is of one and the same nature and substance, not . . . more in all than in each, equally in the Father alone or the Son alone as in the Father and the Son together."[62] "Whatever is . . . said of God himself is said at once triply of the Father and of the Son and of the Holy Spirit and singly of the Trinity itself."[63] The consequence is that the three persons are not only equally related to the one substance, but *identically* related, so that the differences between them, that is, the relations, are irrelevant to their being God. But the original trinitarian insight is that the relations between the identities *are* their being God. When the Nicenes called the Trinity as such God, they so named him *because* of the triune relations and differences; when Augustine calls the Trinity as such God, it is *in spite of* them.

Augustine knew what he was doing. He states the Cappadocian doctrine clearly. Against the Arians, he says, the Nicenes had argued that the Son had to be coeternal with the Father because the Son was the power and wisdom of the Father, so that a Father without the Son would lack essential divine attributes.[64] Augustine then points out that "this reasoning would compel us to say that the Father is not wise except in having the Wisdom he begets, rather than in himself being . . . Wisdom," and similarly for "greatness," "goodness," and so on.[65] Further: "But if nothing is to be said of the Father as such except what is said relatively to the Son . . . , then whatever is said of him, other than that he *is* 'the Father,' is said *with*, or rather *in*, the Son. . . . Thus whatever . . . is said that displays their substance must be said of both *mutually*. . . . For example, the Father must not be called Greatness itself, but the Begetter of greatness; yet neither . . . is the Son great in himself but only *with* the Father whose Greatness he is."[66] Finally: "If things are so, neither is the Father God without the Son nor the Son without the Father; only both mutually are God."[67] This result, says Augustine, is "absurd."[68]

Augustine's description of Nicene teaching is accurate. But what he regards as an unfortunate consequence of the Nicene doctrine was in fact the doctrine's whole original purpose. The original point of trinitarian dialectics is to make the relations between the identities—for example, that the Father's knowledge of himself is what he sees in Jesus—and therewith the temporal structures of evangelical history, constitutive in God. Augustine rejected the Cappadocian doctrine for the sake of his simplicity axiom, which indeed, as he says, makes absurd all talk about the identities only *mutually* being God. And Augustine's position remained axiomatic; Peter Lombard's *Sen-*

tences, the textbook of scholasticism, provides especially blunt formulations, for example, "The Son is indeed called the Wisdom and Power of the Father, but not because the Father is wise and powerful through him, but because the Son is Wisdom and Power from the Father, who is Wisdom and Power. Therefore the Father is not wise by a begotten Wisdom, but by the unbegotten Wisdom he himself is."[69] The *mutual structure* of the identities, relative to the power, wisdom, and so on, that characterize God's work and so God, is flattened into an *identical possession* by the identities of an abstractly simple divine essence.

The original point of trinitarian dogma and analysis was that God's relations to us are internal to him, and it is in carrying out this insight that the "relation" concept was introduced to define the distinction of identities. If God is "one substance," this is a "substance" with internal relations to other substances. But when Western trinitarianism, in arguing how the simplicity of God can be maintained despite the triplicity of persons, uses the relation-concept to show how differences of relation do not necessarily make differences of substance, so that each of the persons "has" the *same* substance, suddenly it is the old notion of substance, defined precisely by *lack* of internal relations, that is assumed. What could and should have been said is that the one and identical Godhead, which each of the persons "has," is itself constituted by the relations between those persons, so that Father, Son, and Spirit play different roles in their joint realization of deity, and just so each possesses the one and selfsame deity.

Nevertheless, with the ambiguity characteristic of Western trinitarianism, the difficult, indeed hopeless, task of thinking the plurality of persons within so abstract an understanding of God's unity compelled Western theology to work out the abstract dialectics of tri-identicality to perfection.[70] Lombard, following Augustine,[71] laid down the dialectical boundary conditions: "The Father is not greater than the Son nor the Father or the Son than the Holy Spirit; nor are two persons together a greater something than one, nor three than two, nor is the divine essence greater in three persons than in two, nor in two than in one."[72] In consequence: "The Father is in the Son and the Son in the Father and the Spirit in both, and each is in each and all."[73] Citing Augustine again: "The Trinity is of one substance, and that essence is not other than the Trinity itself . . . ";[74] ". . . the Father is God, the Son God, the Holy Spirit God; the Father is good, the Son good, and the Holy Spirit good . . . [etc.]; yet there are not three gods or three that are good, but one God, one that is good . . . [etc.]—the Trinity himself."[75] The rule acquired conciliar status: "The three persons are one . . . substance, one essence, one nature, one divinity, one immensity, one eternity; all divine reality is one where an opposition of relation does not prevent it."[76] In particular, it is clear that the three persons of one essence are not to be understood as three things of one stuff, in the manner of Tertullian, or as three that resemble each other fully, after the fashion of Origen, or as three instances of one deity, in the manner of the Cappadocians, or as parts of a whole, in the manner of nobody yet.[77]

In developed Western trinitarianism, distinctions in God are posited by inner divine "processions,"[78] of which there are two: the "begetting" of the Son and the "breathing" of the Spirit.[79] A "procession" is a "movement to an other." The other to which generation and spiration move in God is God himself. Therefore the divine simplicity is supposed not to be violated.[80] Therefore also, since every procession establishes relations, there are relations in God. Moreover, these are "real" relations, that is, not merely external as between two coins possessed by one owner, each of which is the same as if not so related, for since both terms of each such relation are God, the relation cannot be external to its terms.[81]

Two processions immediately give a list of four relations: the Father "begets," the Son "is begotten," the Father and the Son "breathe," and the Spirit "is breathed."[82] And then we have five "notions" applicable to the inner-divine distinctions, the four relations plus "unbegotten" or "unoriginated" of the Father, marking his position as the starting point of all the processions, who himself does not proceed. [83] If now we seek identifying properties for each of the persons, "unoriginated" drops out, since it applies also to the Trinity as such, and so does "breathes," since it applies both to the Father and the Son. Thus, by the sheer geometry of the relational structure, we arrive at exactly three "properties" or "personal notions," one to identify each person: "begets," "is begotten," "is breathed."[84] It surely must be said that the mere aesthetic elegance of this analysis somehow commends it. Figure 1 shows a flow chart of deity.

Then come the great metaphysical assertions. First, the relations and so the personal properties are each identical with the one divine substance "with respect to the entity," that is, as we would say, "objectively," for "paternity" and "breathing forth" are in themselves divine attributes, and each divine attribute, as we have seen, is "with respect to the entity" the divine substance. The relations and properties differ from the divine substance only "with respect to the way we know them," except that "only" is misleading, since this necessity of our knowing is itself founded somehow in the divine reality. The relations and the essence are really the same, but the distinction we cannot help making is necessitated by that one reality.[85]

But if the relations are not merely real in God, but real insofar as and only insofar as they are identical with the divine sub-

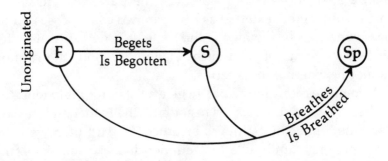

FIGURE 1

stance, then they are real in God in the same way the divine substance is real: they "subsist," that is, they are possessors of attributes (here the divine attributes) and doers of deeds (here the divine deeds). That is, they are proper "persons" in the regular Latin sense of the word.[86] And now, conversely, we can say what the "persons" truly are: " 'Divine person' . . . means *a relation as a subsistent.*"[87]

Within the metaphysical tradition the notion of a subsistent relation—that is, of a relation that can be and *do* things—is of course sheer nonsense. The scholastics labored mightily to mitigate the offense of the notion to what they accepted as natural truth, producing ever more refined distinctions and analyses. But so radical a doctrine of the reality of relations cannot be contained by Plato or Aristotle. That some relations, such as paternity, are founded in the related terms and so have a reality of their own, inherited wisdom can accept. But the trinitarian doctrine identifies the substantiality of the related terms with the internality of the relations between them: there *is*, for example, the Father only because "Father" and "begets" are inseparable. Even the classification of the personal properties to which the scholastics are driven—that they are *both* "relative" and yet "eternal and immutable"[88]—is a defiance of all Hellenic common sense.

This assertion of the substantiality of certain—at least—relations, that is, of their ontological independence and possible priority over against the related terms, is the main place at which the metaphysically revolutionary power of the gospel breaks out in Western theology. In the lead of the Greeks, our inherited ways of thinking suppose that—obviously!—there must first be *things* that in the second place may be variously related. But there is nothing intrinsically obvious about it; in fact, by biblical insight it is the other way around. The general consequences of this reversal of interpretation have long appeared in Western philosophy, most explicitly in some aspects of German idealism, as Hegel's definition of spirit as the relation between self and not-self, which just so is the being of the self. The task of drawing out the more specifically theological consequences has lagged, as it must until the Augustinian doctrine of divine simplicity is discarded. Discarding it is one purpose of this study. We have made various approaches to this objective and will return to it again.

The scholastics fought one significant trinitarian controversy. Are we to say that the Father begets the Son insofar as the Father is identical with the divine substance, or insofar as he is relationally distinct from the other persons? Are we to say that the divine *substance* of the Father begets the divine substance of the Son, or that the relationally constituted *Father* begets the Son *from* his divine substance? Joachim of Fiore asserted the first,[89] Peter Lombard the second.[90] The Fourth Lateran Council of 1215 decided for Lombard,[91] and this was taken for church teaching from then on. We may put the issue thus: Are Father, Son, and Spirit, as repetitions of God, repetitions *of* the divine substance or repetitions *in* the divine substance? Joachim's assertion of the first option is related to his dispensationalism, in which Father, Son, and Spirit each have their period of history, in each of which one divine person rules as God by himself, that is, is the divine substance abstractly from his relations to the other persons. Clearly we must agree with the Lateran Council's choice, but there is also a legitimate concern in Joachim's position, to which we will return.

Despite the brilliance and fruitfulness of the scholastics' trinitarian dialectics, at their heart there remained the old late-antique religious worry about the relation of a supposedly timeless God to his temporal creation. Following Augustine's uncritical return to Greek assumptions, Western theology forbade any assertion about God's relation to time that could suggest change in God himself. That there is a difficulty here, Augustine himself acknowledged: "To see how God . . . creates temporal things and events without any temporal movement of his substance . . . is hard."[92] Nevertheless, Augustine lays down the rule: When we speak of God being our Lord, which he could not be before we existed, or of his becoming our Father at baptism, or of all the like, we must understand that "nothing is added to God, but only to that to which God is said to take up a relation." Thus, for example, "God begins to be our Father when we are reborn. . . . Our substance is changed for the better when we become his children; therewith he also begins to be our Father, *but* without any such change."[93]

The single most disastrous trinitarian result of this rule is that Western teaching, rigorously sorting out usages that had in the East been beneficially vague, makes the trinitarian "processions" in God (i.e., "begetting" and "breathing") and the divine persons' "missions" in time (i.e., the Son's Incarnation and the Spirit's entry into the church; i.e., again, the whole triune reality as Tertullian or Athanasius evoked it) be two simply different and metaphysically separated things: "'mission' and 'sending' . . . are predicated only temporally, 'generation' and 'breathing' only eternally."[94] For since, for example, "generating" happens in God, it cannot be a change, which "sending" clearly is. That the Son is "begotten" by the Father, and that he is "sent" to redeem humanity, are now thought of as distinct realities, one in eternity and other in time: "The Son is said to be sent, not . . . in that he is born of the Father, but either in that he appears in this world as the Word made flesh . . . , or in that he is inwardly apprehended by a temporal mind."[95] Indeed, the way Aquinas seeks to prove that there must be exactly the two processions and no more or others is by saying that the Son emerges by an act of the Father's mind and the Spirit by an act of his will, and that thinking and willing are the only two personal "movements" that do *not* necessarily emerge from the agent, that is, here, from God to a temporal object.[96] In this theology, there are in effect two distinct sets of trinitarian relations, one constituting an "immanent" Trinity, the triune God himself, and the other the "economic" Trinity, the triune pattern of God's work.[97]

The final consequence of these developments is that the trinitarian language of "persons" and "relations" in God loses its original history-of-salvation meaning, and indeed threatens to lose all meaning of any kind. Let me once more state the problem at its simplest. The three derive from God's reality in time, from time's past/present/future. But if the One is one precisely by abstraction from time, the one-and-three can never be made to work. The relations are either *temporal* relations or empty verbiage. In Western trinitarianism, which will not let the relations be temporal, that God is "one and three" becomes the sheer mystification Western churchgoers accept—or reject—it as: something we assert because we are supposed to, not knowing even what we are asserting.

Augustine provided Western theology with a neat formula to sum up the decades of Eastern trinitarian reflection: The Father is God, and the Son is God, and the Spirit is God; and the Father and the Son and the Spirit are not the same one; and the three are but one God. But this formula in its Western actual use no longer represents an activity of analysis to help us understand God. It is instead a paradox formula: Since God is infinite, so that addition and subtraction do not apply, "one is as much as three are together."[98] And with his invariable clarity Augustine sees very well what then happens to the trinitarian language. He explicitly stipulates that when we say one "substance" or three "persons" we communicate nothing whatever, using the words only to say "somehow one" and "somehow three" and using these particular words only because they are traditional.[99] Later theology then makes pious mystery-mongering of the vacuity; for example, it is standard from Lombard on that the Son's "being begotten" differs from the Spirit's "proceeding" only by a difference that cannot be "known in this life."[100] Finally, in Aquinas, the relations have so completely lost their sense as descriptions of saving history's temporal structure that they can differentiate *only* by their geometry; were it not that whereas the Son comes only from the Father, the Spirit comes from both the Father and the Son, Son and Spirit would be the same person.[101]

That the saving works of God, the "works *ad extra*," are works of the whole Trinity no longer can mean that each work is the joint work of Father, Son, and Spirit, in which each identity plays a distinct role, but that the saving works are *indifferently* the work of each person and all. Typically of original Nicene trinitarianism, Basil of Caesarea could say, "When the Father works the various sorts of *events*, and the Son the various sorts of *services*, there is yet the Holy Spirit, who in his own authority manages the distribution of the *charismata* . . . ," and then analyze each work of saving history by this role division.[102] But now the "inseparability" of God's works is identified with the mathematically equal abstract divinity of the triune persons.[103] Creation is undifferentiably the work of the Trinity as one God or of whatever one person you like.[104] And the "sender" of each divine mission is the Trinity, or any of the persons, even including the one sent.[105]

Thus there is no longer any necessary connection between the trinitarian persons and roles or structures of saving history. According to Augustine, the theophanies of the Hebrew Scriptures—the original evidence for the reality of the Logos!—could have been appearances of any trinitarian person, or of the Trinity as such. Only exegesis decides for each instance, and no theological difference is made by the result.[106] Finally, with Lombard it becomes standard for all scholasticism that "just as the Son was made man, so the Father or the Holy Spirit *could* have been and can be now."[107] With this last proposition, the bankruptcy of trinitarian meaning is complete. "The Son" or "the Logos" were originally titles for Jesus in respect of his individual role in God's saving reality. Now they name a pure metaphysical entity, not necessarily related to Jesus at all and—equally with the other divine persons—available for whatever divine duty comes along. Put the disaster thus: As the rule was applied, "The Trinity's works, toward what is outside, are indivisible," *Jesus* and the *church* were taken to be part of "what is outside."

The original meaning of "Father," "Son," "begets," "gift," and so on, as words for the reality of saving history in God, having evaporated, Western theology was compelled to find other meanings for the trinitarian terminology—unless, of course, the whole doctrine was to be abandoned, which was not thinkable before the sixteenth century. Since the relation between creature and God is now back to the old Hellenic standoff between temporality and its negation, also the Hellenic way of giving meaning to talk of timeless deity was inevitably adopted: "Persons" and "relations" are taken to be reality in God describable by *analogy* from temporal reality. The whole pattern of subsequent Western theology is set in the sequence of Augustine's *On the Trinity*. The first seven books analyze inherited trinitarian formulas by the axiom of divine simplicity and end, as we have seen, with their reduction to vacuity.[108] This result demands the search for created analogues of triunity which occupies the remaining books.[109] And the chosen created reality is the human soul, where, from Socrates on, the "image" of timeless deity had chiefly been sought.[110] Therewith the whole relation of God to God's work in time reverted to the pre-Nicene conception of the temporal imaging of timeless reality—Arius was the winner after all.

In Augustine and after, a distinction is made between "visible" and "invisible" missions of the divine persons. It is the visible missions that are the saving history,[111] but the visible missions, so far from themselves being the processions, cannot even, according to Augustine, unambiguously reveal them. If we already have a basis for speaking meaningfully of Father, Son, and Spirit in God himself, we can then see analogies between the visible missions and the processions: "He sends who begets; he is sent who is begotten."[112] And these correspondences are revelatory: "As to be begotten is for the Son to be from the Father, so to be sent is to be known to be from the Father."[113] They enable "appropriations," ways in which in Scripture "in order to suggest the Trinity, some theological predications are made separately of the persons individually named," even though they are not to be understood as actually exclusive predications.[114] So wisdom is attributed to the Son, or love to the Spirit.[115] But we cannot by *these* analogies initially obtain the timeless pole of the analogies, we cannot by them give meaning in the first place to "Father," "Son," and "Spirit," for what saving history teaches us to say of God "is said of God as such, and pertains equally to the whole Trinity, who is one God, and to the several persons. . . . But . . . when or how will the Trinity then appear?"[116] Every event of the evangelical history must be understood as the act of each and all of the persons and of the Trinity as such,[117] down to the slightest detail. Thus, for example, when the Father speaks to the Son at his baptism, a conversation beloved of the old trinitarian exegetes, the speaker is in strict fact no more the Father than the Son or the Spirit or the whole Trinity.[118]

The "invisible" missions constitute that presence of God to the soul which is the possibility of the soul's life, with or without saving history:[119] "[The Word] is then sent to someone, when he is known . . . , insofar as he can be known by a rational soul that is either advancing in God or perfected in God."[120] Knowledge of God is the presence of the Son, and love of God the presence of the Spirit,[121] with or without faith in Christ. It is the great fact and disaster of Western theology that it is *this* reality—which in itself should not be denied—of the soul that knows and wills God, that in Augustine and after[122] is the image of the Trinity by which trinitarian language has meaning, and that the incarnation or the coming of the Spirit to the congregation do *not* achieve this. It is in that God is triune, and in that temporal being is ontologically dependent on inner analogy to timeless being, and in that for the intrinsically self-conscious soul the grasp of this analogy is its own active reality, that we can by analogy to the soul meaningfully say "Father, Son, and Spirit" about God[123]—according to Augustine and his followers.

All temporal being, according to Augustine and his Platonist teachers, is dependent on God in respect of its being, of its intelligibility, and of its activity.[124] The triune image of God in the soul is the realization of these dependences in the mode appropriate to consciousness:[125] "We *are,* we *know* that we are, and we *love* this being and this knowing."[126] And since this self-consciousness is necessarily also God-consciousness,[127] the triple structure of consciousness is an image of divine triplicity: "This . . . trinity of the mind is not the image of God only because the mind remembers itself and knows itself and loves itself, but because it can also remember and know and love the one by whom it is created."[128]

All Augustine's trinitarian analogies, the stock-in-trade of subsequent Western reflection, are but variant descriptions of this structure of simultaneous self- and God-consciousness. The triple dependence is most directly reflected in this formula: being/knowledge/love.[129] Since in the soul's dependence its *being* is love, this formula can turn into: the soul as lover/the soul as object of its own love, that is, as known to itself/the soul as love.[130] The love trinity in its turn, translated into a description of the soul as a substance, becomes: mind/knowledge/love.[131] And translating yet again to a more functional analysis, we get memory/knowledge/will,[132] for the mind as consciousness is identical with itself as being in that it is memory, and love is the action of will. It is by the analogy between God and the soul, analyzed in the last two ways, that Augustine then tries, through the last books of *On the Trinity*, to make trinitarian language work.[133] It may be doubted that he succeeded;[134] whether he did or not, subsequent theology thought he did and followed him.

Our discussion of Western trinitarianism has alternated between lamentation and admiration of the virtues of its defects. We have one more such switch to make. In turning to the soul for a meaning-giving analogue of divine triunity, Augustine necessarily exposed his introspection of the soul to at least some pressure from inherited trinitarian language. Thus he discovered the dialectical complexity of the soul's own reality. That the soul is complex, all antiquity knew. But that the complexity is living and dialectical, that in it each factor is what it is only by and for the other factors, Augustine was first to note: "The soul would not seek to know itself . . . , if it did not in some fashion love itself, with a love which again depends on the knowledge given in memory."[135] In effect, Augustine, looking for analogues of triune deity, discovered the ontological difference of conscious from unconscious being, the great theme of all subsequent Western philosophy.[136] And then Augustine does, however grudgingly, reflect all this back again on God: "Or are we indeed to suppose that the consciousness that God is knows other things and does not know itself . . . ? Behold therefore the Trinity: consciousness, and knowledge of self, and love of self."[137] Several steps removed from authentic trinitarian insight though this interpretation of God is, it is a great intellectual achievement in itself, and one made under the pressure of trinitarian insight. That personal being is an ontological kind of its own, and that God is personal, are deeply Christian notions, and an abiding contribution of Western theology.

Vicissitudes of Western Trinitarianism

The danger of the West's abstract trinitarian analysis is not only that it is false but also that it is likely to reflect negatively upon the fundamental liturgical and proclamatory levels of trinitarian discourse.[138] It seems plain that this has in fact happened, though tracing the history is beyond the scope of this work. One need only think of such phenomena as popular Catholicism's replacement of the triune structure for prayer with one or another piety of the "Jesus-Mary-Joseph" type; or of denominational Lutheranism's centuries-long affection for forms of prayer and praise with only second-article remembrance-content and no invocation of the Spirit; or of Calvinism's concentration of fear and hope upon a pretemporal deity resembling nothing so much as Arius' "Unoriginate." Except at the fringes, the Western church has never entirely lost the trinitarian apprehension, but it is often very close to doing so.

From Augustine on, the doctrine of the Trinity has tended to become increasingly a "revealed Mystery," taught in the proper place of theological systematics because it was supposed to have been supernaturally revealed that God was in fact triune, but having less and less interpretive force for the actual concerns of believers.[139] What was once the explanation has become an item of inherited ideology, itself to be explained as best as possible. As such, it is a setup for destructive critique. The critique has come from both the church and the world.

The doctrine in its Western form has not easily been seen as functional within religious life.[140] Thus one sort of critique, from within the heart of the church, has been benign neglect. The first Reformation system of theology, Melanchthon's *Loci Communes* of 1521, omitted the doctrine altogether, on the grounds that "to know God is to know his benefits," thus clearly supposing that trinitarian discourse is not about God's benefits. Pietists in all branches of the church have regularly taken the same attitude,[141] as did John Locke[142] and other fore-runners of the Enlightenment. Another sort of churchly critique has been more explicit. Western Christians have in effect found themselves, so far as experience is concerned, in a pre-Nicene situation. Many, liberated by historical or philosophical critique from affirming inherited doctrine just because it is inherited, have recapitulated the pre-Nicene theological history, reinventing apologetic subordinationism and Arianism. It is this phenomenon which appears in such "unitarian" movements as have remained Christian: Servetus, the Socinians, or the earlier English and American Unitarians.[143] It appears again in the "neologians," who in Germany mediated the first impact of the Enlightenment.[144] It appears still in various modern critiques, especially in England.[145] Since we have been over that ground once, there is no need to investigate any of these theologies here; we only note their existence and prevalence, then and still.

The full Enlightenment itself, of course, rejected trinitarianism from quite another side. The theological tradition itself posited two bodies of knowledge of God, "natural" and "supernatural," and stipulated the first as that accessible to "reason" and the second as obtained only by bowing to the authority of some agency of revelation. The Enlightenment was a declaration of reason's freedom over against authority; just so it countenanced only the "natural" part of theology. Thus the Enlightenment affirmed Plato's and Aristotle's God in its purity, untouched even by such biblical contaminants as were retained by Augustine.[146] Insofar as the Enlightenment was simply unchurchly, as in France, its unitarianism is outside our story. But insofar as it remained inside the church, as often in England or Germany or the United States, it mingled with such currents as described just before, to promote sundry modalisms and subordinationisms, as well as gentlemanly silent compacts to let sleeping "dogmatic" dogs lie.

Under all these kinds of critique the inherited doctrine of the Trinity was by the opening of the nineteenth century nearly defunct in those parts of the church open to modernity. But the history of nineteenth-century spirituality and theology—at least in such parts of the church—was a series of attempts to "overcome the Enlightenment" with respect to its evacuation of religious substance, without returning to reliance on supernatural authority. Two great figures dominate the effort, Friedrich Schleiermacher and G. F. W. Hegel, and both are important for current trinitarian thought. Schleiermacher typifies and largely inaugurated the dominant pattern, which gets along without much trinitarianism. Hegel deliberately "renewed" the doctrine as a speculative insight, providing the pattern of other such attempts thereafter and much of the impetus and conceptual style for the more churchly twentieth-century renewal by Karl Barth.

Schleiermacher put his exceedingly brief section on the Trinity at the end of his systematics, as a kind of summary. There it cannot function to identify the God spoken of in the body of the work. Rather, having expounded what is effectively the contents of a three-article creed, Schleiermacher then takes such a creed's "Father . . , Son . . , Spirit" as a concluding memory-device suggested by tradition. At the level of the immediate expression and critique of piety, the doctrine's necessary function, he says, is to insist "that nothing less than the divine being was in Christ and inhabits the Christian church as its communal spirit, and that we do not take these expressions in any weakened sense . . . and intend to know nothing of . . . subordinate divinities."[147] To that we must say, so far so good.

As a doctrine about the "divine being" itself, however, the doctrine of the Trinity is, according to Schleiermacher, a bungle. Such doctrine first results from "eternalizing the distinction between the being of God for itself and the being of God for the unification [with Jesus and the church]."[148] But just that move is disastrous. Schleiermacher's critique, it is vital to note, is precisely that which Augustine directed against the Cappadocians:[149] the illegitimacy of saying anything material of only one person. And the root of the critique is also the same: uncritical acceptance of the Greek dogma that divinity equals timelessness:[150] "the divine causality [Schleiermacher's interpretation of God's reality] . . . must be conceived as utterly timeless." The result is also the same, that God is spoken of only by negative analogies: "This is achieved through expressions which name temporal reality and is therefore achieved by pictures: . . . one equates the temporal opposites of before-and-after, earlier-and-later, and so suspends them."[151]

But where Augustine struggled to maintain some sense for the inherited trinitarian propositions, Schleiermacher just drops them. He is free to do this because, according to him, specifically Christian apprehension does not reach to the basic understanding of God at all; this is borrowed (his word) from universally valid philosophical analysis.[152] Thus Schleiermacher maintains, despite what is usually said of him, a particularly simpleminded form of the disastrous old distinction of natural from revealed theology.

If, for reasons of purely intellectual harmonization, we still want a doctrine of triunity, Schleiermacher has two recommendations. First, the doctrine should be "Sabellian," a description of successive temporal manifestations of a divine reality itself unaffected thereby. Second, we should take "the Father" as a name for this divine reality, and "the Son" and "the Spirit" as names for the manifestations.[153] Thus Schleiermacher's recommendation is exactly and compendiously Arian after all.

We need not decide whether Schleiermacher's version of the Trinity has greatly influenced nineteenth- and twentieth-century ordinary Christianity, or only marvelously exemplifies it. It is enough to note that most Protestant readers will recognize in the last paragraphs a description of what they gleaned from the catechetics and preaching of "main-line" denominations.

Hegel[154] deliberately set out to reinvigorate the inherited doctrine of the Trinity by releasing its metaphysically revolutionary implications. He made the Augustinian-Western version of the doctrine the center of his philosophy, the West's last universal and perhaps last great system of thought. Augustine, we have insisted, failed to describe a genuinely tri-identical God, but in the attempt he did perceive new truth. He perceived a *personal*, in the modern sense, God, whose being is constituted in the inner dialectics of consciousness: in the play of—now we will use the language of Hegel's time—immediate self-consciousness (Augustine's "memory"), objective knowledge of self, and freedom that unites them. Hegel abandoned Augustine's hesitations, made this interpretation a universal concept of personal being, and then made all reality personal.

It was Hegel's goal to make a true synthesis of the two clashing streams of Western thought: the Greek will rationally to grasp reality's sense, and the Bible's grasp of reality as history, with all history's contingencies and contradictions. This can be done, said Hegel, if we see that history makes its *own kind* of sense, which is the sense not of the merely beholding and sense-describing mind, but of the living and sense-creating spirit. The spirited rationality of poets and great statesmen—and of authentic philosophers like Plato—does not abstract from contingency and contradictions, only so to achieve itself; it posits them, to overcome and encompass them and so achieve an expanding, living meaning. Napoleon does not abhor enemies; he seeks them, to create a larger European order in the struggle. Goethe does not banish irrationality and conflict from his plots; he invents them, to achieve the meaning of drama rather than of mere chronicle. Abstractly stated: the rational subject posits the object, that is, that which is not itself, is not sheer transparent meaning; then the rational subject achieves itself as the *process*, the *act*, of rediscovering itself in the object, that is, of finding meaning in what is not merely as such meaningful; this event of reconciliation between reason-as-subject, and object-made-reasonable is living reason, spirit.

Since reality is historical, it is the sort of sense just described that reality has: the eternal creating and overcoming of contradiction in higher harmony. Since reality has this sort of sense, true reason is the mind that fulfills itself as just described, that works out its own reason precisely in contradictory and contingent objects. The great metaphysical claim follows of itself: reality-as-history makes sense only as the object of a Subject that finds itself therein, and so is itself Spirit. God is Thinker; and he is Thought; and finally he is the Act of the Thinker finding himself in what is thought, so that this *is* indeed *thought*. God is the Mind that has the world for object; he is the world insofar as Mind indeed finds sense, and so Itself, in the world; and he is the free Spirit that occurs as this event. God is the absolute Statesman-Poet-Philosopher. God is just what Augustine said: Mind and Knowledge and Love that joins them.

Hegel believed Western thought fulfilled itself with him; at least so far as its trinitarianism is concerned, he was right. Augustine's insight can be taken no further. Neither can Augustine's failure: this trinitarianism's distance from the saving history that necessitates trinitarianism in the first place. In Hegel, Augustinian trinitarianism fulfills its constant tendency by finally explicitly taking the world as God's Object, rather than Jesus. And from Hegel on there has been a tradition in which the trinitarian dialectics are frankly exploited for their speculative possibilities, and without much direction of the speculation by those dialectics' original object, the events with Christ. Perhaps the most notable recent exponents of this tradition are John Macquarrie and Paul Tillich.[155] I, of course, must regard their efforts as the perfecting of ancient error.

The modern Western church has thus repeated the confrontation with an again independent Hellenism. The result to date much resembles the penultimate result of the first confrontation. Where the faith is lively, believers—the previous trinitarian heritage being now mostly inaccessible to them—fall back on perennial modalism and simply think of Jesus as their God or as part of God. Learned theology, and the theology of those congregations most alienated from the faith, is Arian.

It is possible that this time the confrontation is lost, so that the Western church cannot maintain an interpretation of God by the gospel, cannot survive as specifically Christian. If there is hope, it can only be in a yet more radical trinitarianism than the first time around.

The beginning, anyway, has been made: Karl Barth[156] has reachieved an authentic doctrine of tri-unity by what amounts to a christological inversion of Hegel's. Only put *Jesus* in place of Hegel's "world," and you have the doctrine of Barth's *Church Dogmatics*, volume 1/1—which observation takes nothing from the extraordinary ingenuity of Barth's move. For the rest, there are two aspects of Barth's doctrine which we must explicitly note.[157]

First, Barth perceives the difference between the Hellenic quest for God (he says "natural theology") and the gospel's proclamation that Jesus is God's quest for us (he says "revelation") more rigorously than any before him (except Luther?) and uses this insight as the sole motor of trinitarian discourse. The entire doctrine of the Trinity, he says, is but the specification of which God it is that *can* so reveal himself as in fact happens with Christ.[158]

The biblical claim of revelation, Barth says, poses three questions: Who is revealed? What does he do to reveal himself? What does revelation accomplish?[159] And the answer to each must be "God," without qualification:[160] "*God* reveals himself. He reveals himself *through himself.* He reveals *himself.*"[161] And apart from each of these three sentences, the other two remain ambiguous.[162] The key point is why the answer to all three questions must be simply "God." Summarizing drastically, we may state Barth's answer: in order to negate our religious quest conceptually, to fit the way in which revelation in Jesus' death and resurrection actually negate it.[163] If the revelation, Jesus, or the achievement of revelation, the divine Spirit among us, were not simply God himself, we would by them merely be launched on a religious quest for God himself. But what the cross and resurrection reveal is exactly that such a quest denies the sufficiency of the word of the gospel and therefore is unbelief. Yet the God *who* so reveals himself does not thereby become merely identical with the historical revelation and thereby accomplished presence; that God is never thus grasped by us is, again, what the cross reveals. Therefore also the one revealed is God utterly.

Having thus prevented subordinationism, Barth excludes modalism by the very same consideration. The necessity of giving the same answer to all three of revelation's questions does not amalgamate the questions themselves into one, for then again the real God would remain behind revelation and we would be back on our quest.

Second, in Barth's conduct of trinitarian analysis—in which

he is able to adapt most of the tradition—the key notions are those of "act" and "repetition." He can summarize the positions we have just sketched thus: The doctrine of the Trinity is to make clear that as "Father, Son, and Spirit, God is *our* God antecedently in himself."[164] But that means that God is action and relatedness antecedently in himself, that he is history antecedently in himself.[165] The divine being is that very lordship that occurs in God's act of triune revelation.[166] And the threeness in God must therefore be understood not as three instances of one deity but as three events of one deity:[167] God *is* God, and then *is* God again and again, each time in a different way.[168] Barth's entire position can be stated in one sentence: "The name of Father, Son, and Spirit says that God is the one God in a triple repetition, and in such a way that this repetition itself is grounded in his deity, that is, in such a way that . . . only in this repetition is he the one God."[169] Only by this repetition is God so present to us that we can in no way get past him, and just this inescapability is his lordship, that is, his deity.[170]

Because it is Barth who taught twentieth-century theology—or the lively parts of it—the importance and point of trinitarian discourse, his influence has been pervasive through this entire study, and that must here be explicitly acknowledged. But his contribution to required new trinitarian *analysis* is not so great as might be expected, nor does he carry us to full liberation from a past-determined interpretation of God.[171] There is room for further reflection.

Proposals

Trinitarian analysis is by no means complete, nor will it be until the struggle between the gospel's and Hellenism's identifications of God is over—which will be when the Western church is over or the world is over. It is time to state such of my own proposals as are not yet explicit.[172]

The first step is to free trinitarian doctrine from captivity to antecedent interpretation of deity as timelessness.[173] In part that is already done in this work—as in Barth and some other post-Hegelian treatments—by the mere sequence of topics and by the christological concentration I, again like Barth, have insisted on at every step.

Within the trinitarian dialectics themselves it is the relation of the "immanent" and "economic" Trinities that must in this connection be reconsidered. Historical justice requires us to note that just such a reconsideration was begun by those theologians who tried to carry the insights of the Reformation into speculative theology, the Lutheran "scholastics" of the seventeenth century.[174] In the final systems of this movement, the rigid Augustinian separation of "externally directed" and "internally directed" works of the Trinity is broken by an elaborate set of further divisions. The "externally directed" works are now, as acts, some external and some internal, so that we now think of events *in* God that have exterior results as their aim. Among the wholly "external" works, there appear certain distinct works of the three persons, occurring in those biblical conversations between Jesus and his Father in their Spirit, as at Jesus' baptism, that were beloved of the Nicene trinitarians. And most important, the "missions" of the Son and the Spirit, precisely as they are done "in time," are here classed as "internally directed."[175]

The trinitarian revisions of the Lutheran scholastics remained at the level of paradox, or even mere inconsistency, and their whole style of theology was swept away by the Thirty Years' War and by the trinitarian indifference and critique of pietism and Enlightenment. We may therefore turn directly to the contemporary task. The two most important contemporary trinitarian theorists, Karl Rahner and Eberhard Jüngel, agree on the rule for that task: the "economic" Trinity *is* the "immanent" Trinity, and vice versa, thereby bluntly stating what the old Lutherans were gingerly approaching.[176]

The legitimate theological reason for the "immanent"/"economic" distinction is the freedom of God: it must be that God "in himself" could have been the same God he is, and so triune, had there been no creation, or no saving of fallen creation, and so also not the trinitarian history there has in fact been. Here is a second rule. Reconciling it with the one just stated has always been the problem.

The two rules are compatible, I propose, only if the identity of the "economic" and "immanent" Trinity is *eschatological*, if the "immanent" Trinity is simply the eschatological reality of the "economic." In captivity to the timelessness-axiom, the tradition could conceive the eternity of Jesus only by positing a reality that always *was* in God. Thus was posited the "Logos *asarkos*," the "not [yet] incarnate Word," who always was in God and then *became* the one sent in flesh to us. The Logos' relation to the Father was described as a Father-Son relation, and rightly, since it is Jesus' relation to his Father that is to be interpreted. But the begetting and being-begotten of *this* Father and *this* Son had to be timeless; thus this "procession" could not in fact be the same as the temporal relation of Jesus to his Father, that is, as the "mission." The Greek fathers mostly ignored the difficulty, thus permitting authentic trinitarian discourse in which the processions and missions occur together.[177] But when more rigid thinkers came along, the difficulty proved fatal. This whole pattern must be reversed.

Instead of interpreting Christ's deity as a separate entity that always *was*—and preceding analogously with the Spirit—we should interpret it as a final *outcome*, and just *so* as eternal, just so as the bracket around all beginnings and endings. Jesus' historical life was a sending by the Father; a filial relation between Jesus and the Transcendence to which he turned temporally in fact occurred. And this man is risen from the dead, so that his mission must triumph, so that his filial relation to his Father is unimpeachable. Thus Jesus' obedience to the Father, and their love for us which therein occurs, *will* prove unsurpassable events, which is the same as that they now *are* God-events, "processions" in God. Jesus' Aramaic or Hebrew prayer, and his prophetic apprehension of God's word, will be the Father's final Self-Expression, by which he establishes his identity for us and for himself. And the spirit that is the breath of this Future will blow all things before himself into new life. That is, the saving events, whose plot is stated by the doctrine of trinitarian relations, *are*, in their eschatological finality, God's transcendence of time, his eternity, so that we need posit no timelessly antecedent extra entities—Logos *asarkos* or not-yet-given Spirit—to assert the unmitigated eternity of Son and Spirit.

Within trinitarian thought's captivity to an alien definition of deity, we have been unable to say simply that Jesus *is* "the eternal Son," that what happens between the human Jesus and his Father and the believing community *is* eternity. Instead, to assert the Son's eternity, we have had to say that Jesus is the dwelling and manifestation of his own preexistent Double— and with that all the impossibilities we have trudged through present themselves. It is the need for the "pre-" that causes them; that is, it is the interpretation of eternity as Persistence of the first past that causes them. If we instead follow Scripture in understanding eternity as Faithfulness to the last future, these problems disappear—whatever others may appear.

Truly, the Trinity is simply the Father and the man Jesus and their Spirit as the Spirit of the believing community. This "economic" Trinity is *eschatologically* God "himself," an "immanent" Trinity. And that assertion is no problem, for God *is* himself only eschatologically, since he is Spirit.

As for God's freedom, only this proposal fully asserts it. The immanent Trinity of previous Western interpretation had but the spurious freedom of unaffectedness. Genuine freedom is the reality of possibility, is openness to the future; genuine freedom is Spirit. And it is only if we interpret God's eternity as the certainty of his triumph that we are able without qualification to say that God is Spirit. If we so understand God's freedom, we are indeed unable to describe *how* God could have been the selfsame triune God other than as the "economic" Trinity now in fact given. But neither have we any call to, so long as God's utter freedom, as Spirit, is acknowledged. In that acknowledgment we are equally commanded to say *that* God could be otherwise the triune God and forbidden to say how.

Therewith we are at the next required amendment of inherited teaching. On a traditional diagram of trinitarian relations, the procession of divine being is all one way, from the Father. Son and Spirit derive their deity from the Father, but Father and Son do not derive deity from the Spirit: "the Father is the principle and source of the whole of deity."[178] The places for relations whose arrows would point *to* the Father are vacant.

Pre-Nicene subordinationism had two closely related roots. One was the need for mediation of time and eternity. The other was the apprehension of God as fundamentally located at the Beginning rather than the End, so that the trinitarian relations, even when rightly set parallel to time, had as active relations to point only *with* time's arrow. It corresponded to this apprehension that to command, beget, give, and so on,[179] were felt as more appropriate to deity than to be given, obey, and the like. Of these two sorts of subordinationism, only the first was overcome by the Cappadocians. Thus it became a fixed axiom that the Father's begetting marked a sole primacy in deity,[180] that the Transcendence to whom Jesus looked back was actively deity, while the Spirit he gave to the future was only passively so.

The asymmetry of the trinitarian relations is the more remarkable in that the Bible clearly presses candidates for the missing parts of the diagram. I propose to fill them in. Which items of biblical language we choose for the future-to-past active relations is of secondary importance. Using "witnesses" for the Spirit and "frees" for the Spirit with the Son, we may say: The Spirit's witness to the Son, and the Son's and the Spirit's joint reality as the Openness into which the Father is freed from mere persistence in his pretemporal transcendence, are equally God-constituting with the traditional relations. And that the only biblical approach to a definition of deity is "God is Spirit" demands that the Spirit be recognized as differently but equally "principle and source" with the Father; let us mark this with a "notion," and let that be "unsurpassed." Thus we obtain the new diagram shown in Figure 2.

The tradition could say how sending and obedience, giving and being given, are realities not merely between God and us, but in God—and so final goods. But it could not say how freeing and being freed, witnessing and being witnessed to, are equally realities in God. Thus the tradition could show that—to use Reformation language—God's *law* is his own true self-expression. But it could not show that the *gospel* is similarly anchored in God's being. I do not suggest that the church so

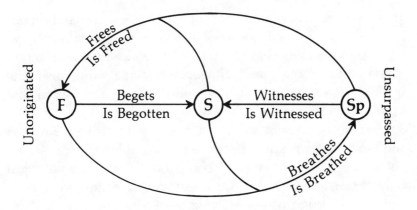

FIGURE 2

persistently slides into legalism because of gaps in a diagram; I do suggest that it does so because of a conception of God accurately represented by the traditional diagram, by which God in himself is indeed God of the law but not of the gospel, defined in his deity by command but not by promise. I wish to amend the conception.

Again, that the gospel is to be a word of liberation is now suddenly affirmed by theologians of all sorts. How could it have been so long unrecognized? The "liberation theologians" did not, after all, invent the massive biblical testimony, for it was there all along. And how does it happen that most pious Christians still regard liberations as threats to faith, or that so many launched by faith on actual works of liberation are thereby led out of faith? Again, I do not suggest that people about to do something liberating check with a theology text and are put off by trinitarian discrepancies. But I do suggest that the textbooks reflect habits of speech about God that are deeply ingrained in the discourse of the church and that simply do not present him as an overly plausible liberator.[181]

Finally, on this line, this is the place where the traditional doctrine of God does indeed reflect male chauvinism. Whether or not dominance is biologically a male characteristic, it has been culturally. The traditional asymmetry of the trinitarian relations, by which deity runs only one way, displays command as constitutive of deity, but not obedience, assertion but not reception. Indeed, the very definition of deity as assertion against time and its chances, which lies behind the asymmetry of relations and against which we have been arguing, bears the same value preference. It has been convincingly argued that these characteristics of traditional trinitarianism are the last outpost of the ancient world's dominance of active male solar and sky gods over passive female earth and lunar gods.[182] I do not suggest that the ancient correlation of male/female with active/passive is true. Nor do we propose recognition of symmetry in the inner-triune derivations of deity, in order to "emphasize the female" or something of the sort. The point is rather to eliminate altogether any inheritances from antiquity's polytheistic distinction of male and female deity, and from its attribution of dominance to the male.

With the essentiality of God's reality as Spirit finally stated, we are in a position to consider again the Augustinian-Hegelian discovery of God's personhood, in the modern sense. God, we may summarize their doctrine, is himself as Subject; is himself his own Object, to be self-consciousness; and, discovering *himself* as object, *is* himself only as the occurrence of this discovery, to be Spirit. Just and only so, God is personal. The great failure of this insight is that the dynamic dialectic of personhood is understood as entirely contained *in* God, who "toward what is outside" is still a pure monad, only giving hints of his internal liveliness by analogues in creation.[183] Just so, the Hellenic interpretation of eternity as timelessness is not ultimately abandoned. The self-achievement of consciousness—whether in God or in us—is still understood as the realization of possibilities in there from the beginning. And consciousness can be absolute in God, and be the analogue of absolute consciousness in us, in that it is *self*-consciousness, in that it is finally independent and self-maintaining, that is, in that it is consciousness-as-substance.

But surely it is just from trinitarian doctrine itself that we should learn that a personal self is not a monad, that its "internal" dynamic structure is inseparable from its relations to other selves, that personhood is intrinsically a communal phe-

nomenon. I—and God!—am the *person* that I am precisely in
that *you* intrude into my life, opening me to be what I am not
yet in what would be my self were I not personal. It is the
communality of God's and our personhood that we have yet
to grasp.[184]

By the resurrection the Father makes Jesus' personal intention, defined—as is every personal intention—by his particular
life and death, unsurpassable. That is, now bringing ourselves
and our religious need into the story, by the resurrection the
Father proposes Jesus' person to us as that to which we may
finally look forward. That is, again, the Father proposes Jesus
as that to which we may look to be looking to God. Jesus is
the object we have in knowing God.

Personal presence and so personal knowledge occur always
as address, always as the word-event by which one person
enters the reality of another. This entrance may be destructive,
it may initiate a relation of dominance and subservience, and
a struggle over who will have which. If there is such a struggle,
the outcome will be that one of us, as we say, makes a mere
object of the other, that one is only a subject for the other, who
is only an object for him. It is often carelessly supposed that
what should instead happen is that neither is object for the
other, that a "pure" I-Thou relation occurs. But that is clearly
impossible. If I address you, I merely thereby make you my
object. If I do not seek by my address to enslave you, what I
must do is so address you as to grant myself also as your
object. I must appear in your world as a possible target of your
intention: as a describable and so identifiable reality, as a reality
about which you can make choices and upon whom you can
act, as an item in your time. True mutuality is *mutual* self-
objectification.

God's address to us in the gospel is liberating and not en-
slaving. Therefore his presence must grant us an object to
which we may attend, and in attending to which we may intend God. Jesus is the object and his resurrection is the grant.

Next step: That this revelation is *true*, that in knowing and
willing Jesus we finally and unconditionally know and will
God, that the gospel involves no "ifs," means that this objec-

tivity holds also for God, that in knowing and willing Jesus, God knows and wills himself. The object to which we look as we attend to the gospel, the temporal Jesus, is the same object that God intends in the "immanent" self-consciousness that is his life. As God turns to himself, he turns to Jesus the Nazarene. Just so, the temporal Jesus is a second identity in God, without need for a metaphysical double; and God has himself as his own Object, to be personal being and so to be Spirit.

To see, next, how personal reality, including God's, is a communal phenomenon, we must ask how it can happen that I have myself as my own object. Surely the directly plausible account must be: *You* have me for your object within our mutual address and response, and if by our discourse we in fact come to communicate, to share a world, I share also your objective apprehension of myself. That I have myself as my own object is thus communally mediated. Nor is there reason not to adopt this initially plausible account, since traditional accounts that omit your role in my personhood and posit an "immediate self-consciousness" seem to have no other reason than the advance conviction that also personal beings *must* be substances, constituted in themselves. There is no reason to maintain this prejudice.

In the biblical proclamation there indeed is no reason to deny that also *God* is constituted as personal in his community with us. The one in whom the Father intends himself is Jesus, an item of and subject in our history. And it is for our believing community that Jesus and his Father have one Spirit.

But we do still want to say that God could have been God without us. How can we, if community with us constitutes his triunity?

What must be grasped—and this is the highest pitch of trinitarian analysis—is that God could have been also *communal* without us, that in his eschatological immanence he would finally be "we" with or without creatures. And that can, in a fashion, be grasped—though, again, only *that* it is so, not *how* it is so. For although the triune identities are not, as such, persons in the modern sense, God is; and if each identity is God, each identity is also personal, and the three a community.

"The wonder of God's inner trinitarian life is that the numerically single personal 'I' of the one being that God is . . . has his being only in the true community of a personal 'we.'" "The basic meaning of the begetting of the Son is that God posits community in himself."[185]

I can say "I" only over against a "you." But you are also an "I." Over against what "you" are you are an "I"? Not over against me, for then the relation would be self-sustaining, which creatures are not. Over against a third party, then, and so on, so that the ground of my reality as "I" disappears into an infinite series. It is the very mark of God that it does not happen so with him: The Father is "I" over against the Son as "you"—who is the same "I" the Father is, and yet a genuine "you," so God could have been community for himself.[186]

I can now conclude by tidying up my proposal about the trinitarian relations. If we, following Augustinian-Hegelian insight, substitute the more accurate "intends" for the traditional "begets" and the less metaphorical "gives" for "breathes," we can draw a diagram as in Figure 3.

There are then ten "notions" and eight "relations." The relations will not reduce to three "properties" by the medieval principle alone. But if we take the relations in pairs, using the active relations for the Father and the Spirit and not duplicat-

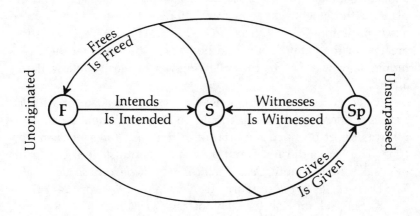

FIGURE 3

ing, we get: the Father gives and intends, the Spirit frees and witnesses, Jesus is intended and is witnessed to. And interpreting each pair personally, we get: the Father gives and intends = is Subject; Jesus is intended and is witnessed to = is Object; the Spirit frees and witnesses = is Spirit.

NOTES

1. Athanasius *Letter to Serapion IV* 4.3.

2. Origen *Commentary on Romans (EnchP 502)*, 7.13; *Commentary on John* 2.10.75.

3. *Conciliorum Oecumenicorum Decreta* (Freiburg: Herder, 1973), p. 28.

4. Athanasius *Discourse Against the Arians III* (PG 26:321–467), 65.

5. The favorite creed of all anti-*homoousian* wings, except the most extreme Arians, was the so-called Creed of Lucian; see Philip Schaff, ed., *The Creeds of Christendom* (New York: Harper & Row, 1877), 2:27: "the [biblical] names were not given at random, but precisely signify the proper hypostasis and rank and glory of each of those named. Thus they are three by hypostasis but one by harmony." As for the Arians themselves, see Arius *Letter to Alexander*, in Gustave Bardy, *Recherches sur Saint-Lucien d'Antioch et son École* (Paris: Beauchesne, 1936), pp. 235–36: "hoste treis eisin hypostaseis."

6. This was clearly seen by Basil, who noted that the Latins were obliged to translate both *ousia* and *hypostaseis* by *substantia* and applauded those who gave up translation and simply transliterated *ousia*; Basil the Great *Letters* (PG 32:219–1114), 214.4. Augustine, greatest of the Latins, confessed he had no idea of what the Greek terminology was for. In the following, I will mostly follow Basil's advice.

7. The Greeks sometimes used *prosopon* instead of or with *hypostasis*. *Prosopon* and *persona* should be close equivalents. But *prosopon* was never of much importance in the East, for trinitarian doctrine. The Latins did not adopt *persona* as its translation, but for its own sake. René Braun, *Deus Christianorum: Recherches sur le Vocabulaire Doctrinal de Tertullien* (Paris: Universitaire, 1967), pp. 24–242.

8. See Helmut Koester, "Hypostasis," *ThWNT* 8:571–78.

9. The language group here is a variety of expressions with *idios* and its derivatives; see the listings in *Index Aristotelicus*, ed. H. Bonitz (Darmstadt: Wissenschaftliche Buchgesellschaft, 1960 [reissue]), p.

339. Thus in Aristotle's *Prior Analytics* A27, the premises of argument are required to have predicates *hosa idia tou pragmatos esti.* It is this language group the Cappadocians will use to elucidate *hypostasis.*

10. Joseph Owens, *The Doctrine of Being in the Aristotelean Metaphysics* (Toronto: Pontifical Institute of Mediaeval Studies, 1951), pp. 307–99; Klaus Kremer, *Die Neuplatonische Seinsphilosophie und ihre Wirkung auf Thomas von Aquin* (Leiden: Brill, 1966), pp. 79–138; Werner Marx, *The Meaning of Aristotle's "Ontology"* (The Hague: Nijhoff, 1954), pp. 22–64.

11. E.g., Basil the Great *Letters* 214.

12. E.g., Gregory of Nyssa *Against Eunomius,* in his *Opera,* vol. 1–2, ed. W. Jaeger (Leiden: Brill, 1960), 1.227.

13 E.g., Gregory Nazianzus *Orations* 31.9; Gregory of Nyssa *Eunomius* 1:278–80.

14. Gregory of Nyssa *To Ablabius: That There Are Not Three Gods,* in his *Opera,* vol. 3/1, ed. F. Müller (Leiden: Brill, 1958), 117.

15. Gregory Nazianzus *Orations* 31.15–16; Gregory of Nyssa *To the Greeks, from Shared Notions,* in his *Opera,* vol. 3/1, ed. F. Müller (Leiden: Brill, 1958), pp. 20–25; *Against Eunomius* 1.167–69, 231–37, 270–76; 3/3.10; 1/180–86.

16. Basil the Great *Against Eunomius* 2.22; Gregory Nazianzus *Orations* 34.10.

17. Gregory of Nyssa *Ablabius* 135.

18. According to ibid. there are three ontological questions: "Is it?" "What is it?" "How is it?" The distinction of the three hypostases is only "with respect to *how* it is."

19. Thomas Aquinas *Summa Theologica* 1.29.3–4.

20. This is true even in detail; e.g., Basil the Great *On the Holy Spirit* (PG 32:67–218), 61–64.

21. It is here worth noting a confirmation of a main thesis of this book, that the trinitarian dialectics are to resist assimilation of the gospel's God to more normal identifications of God. Christopher B. Kaiser, "The Ontological Trinity in the Context of Historical Religions," *SJTh* 29 (1976): 301–10, points out that the supposed three-hypostases parallels in other religions are *all* to subordinationism or modalism, since they are all projections toward the world from a distant God, along a hierarchy of being vertical to time, while in the proper doctrine of the Trinity the hypostases and their relations are perpendicular to the God-creation relation. Father, Son, and Spirit are *together* both immanent and transcendent; for this, Kaiser finds no parallels, nor do I know of any.

22. E.g., Gregory Nazianzus *Orations* 31.8, 16.

23. Or alternatively, the incarnation is the mediation, not the Logos as such. See Gregory of Nyssa *Refutation of Eunomius' Confession* 144, in his *Opera*. Here is the origin of what was to be the orthodox christology.

24. Further on to this sort of reflection, Eberhard Jüngel, *The Doctrine of the Trinity* (Grand Rapids: Eerdmans, 1976).

25. E.g., Gregory Nazianzus *Orations* 31.8. Gregory finally denies all models of the Trinity, except homiletically; ibid., 31–33.

26. Ekkehard Mühlenberg, *Die Unendlichkeit Gottes bei Gregor von Nyssa* (Göttingen: Vandenhoeck & Ruprecht, 1966). For earlier theological use of "infinite," see Werner Elert, *Der Ausgang der altkirchlichen Christologie* (Berlin: Lutherisches Verlagshaus, 1957), pp. 37–53.

27. Gregory of Nyssa *Against Eunomius* 1.291, 368.

28. Ibid., 1.684.

29. Ibid., 2.104–5.

30. Gregory Nazianzus is especially insistent that none of the negative predicates of Platonic theology has any more application to the being or subsistence of God than do their affirmative correlates; *Orations* 28.9.

31. Gregory of Nyssa *Against Eunomius* 2.34.

32. E.g., Gregory of Nyssa *Refutation of Eunomius* 3–8, 14.

33. Ibid., 15.

34. Gregory of Nyssa *Ablabius* 121.

35. Ibid.

36. Ibid., 124. Or see *Against Eunomius* 2.102.

37. Gregory of Nyssa *Ablabius* 124; *Against Eunomius* 2.149.

38. Gregory of Nyssa *Ablabius* 125.

39. Gregory Nazianzus *Orations* 31.14.

40. Augustine *On the Trinity* 1.7.

41. Ibid., 5.10.

42. In the following I use *Against Eutyches and Nestorius*.

43. Aquinas *Summa* 1.19.1–2.

44. Here *mens* = *nous*.

45. Augustine *Confessions* 7.10.

46. Ibid. See Olivier du Roy, *L'intelligence de la Foi en la Trinité selon Saint Augustin* (Paris: Études Augustiniennes, 1966), pp. 109–206.

47. Augustine *Confessions* 7.10. Nor did this structure disappear from Augustine's mature thought; e.g., *Trinity* 13.3.

48. Augustine *Confessions* 7.18.

49. E.g., Augustine *On Order* 6.26; *Trinity* 4.26.

50. This and the above has been minutely argued by du Roy, *L'intelligence;* see esp. pp. 25–106, 117–124, 215, and the summaries on pp. 413–19, 453–56. We must note that in the individual matters for which I will criticize Augustine he had predecessors; Jean-Louis Maier, *Les Missions Divines selon Saint Augustin* (Freiburg: University, 1960), pp. 199–219. It is the ensemble that makes the difference.

51. When in the following my polemic is all aimed at the West, this does not mean I think the later Eastern development was in order, only that it is outside the scope of my investigation. Indeed, the recapitulation and perpetuation of late-antique paganism seems to be more abject in the East, with the reception in the fourteenth century of the teaching of Gregory Palamas, who simply replaces the function of the economic Trinity with divine cosmic and social "energies" of the purest gnostic character. For description, see A. M. Ammann, *Die Gotteschau im palamitischen Hesychasmus* (Rome: Pontifical Institute, 1939), and Leon A. Zander, "Die Weisheit Gottes im russischen Glauben und Denken," *KuD* 2 (1956): 29–53.

52. Thus Aquinas *Summa* 1.2–26 discusses the existence, simplicity, perfection, goodness, infinity, relation to creatures, changelessness, eternity, unity, truth, names, knowledge, life, will, love, justice, mercy, providence, foreknowledge, power, and blessedness of God before making any reference to his triunity.

53. Augustine *Studies in the Gospel of John* 1.8. Aquinas' procedure is the same: *Summa* 1.2.3.

54. Augustine *John* 38.10.

55. Augustine *Trinity* 5.2; *City of God* 5.10.

56. Augustine *Commentary on the Psalms* 2.10; Aquinas *Summa* 2.13.11.

57. Augustine *On the Customs of the Catholic Church and of the Manichaeans* 1.1.14; Aquinas *Summa* 1.13.aa. To all this paragraph, see Axel Dahl, *Augustin und Plotin* (Lund: University, 1945), pp. 8–9.

58. Augustine *Trinity* 5.3.

59. Aquinas *Summa* 1.3.6.

60. Augustine *Trinity* 5.11. According to the nation of substance, it *should* be so with all substances, i.e., for the author of this note to be a man and for him to be rational, etc., should be the same. It is just the fact that it is not so, the Lockean possibility of peeling attributes from created substances down to a "substance" that is finally

no more than a something-we-know-not-what, that marks the defective substantiality of all but God, the penetration of temporality into these substances themselves.

61. Augustine *City* 1.11.10.1. The simplicity of God is the first divine attribute discussed by Aquinas and made to be the basis of all the others; *Summa* 1.3.

62. Augustine *Letters* 170.5

63. Augustine *Trinity* 5.9.

64. Ibid., 5.1.

65. Ibid., 5.2.

66. Ibid., 7.1–2.

67. Ibid., 5.3.

68. Ibid., 7.2. Alfred Schindler, *Wort und Analogie in Augustins Trinitaetslehre* (Tübingen: J. C. B. Mohr, 1965), p. 165. Note that this argument depends on the identity of being God with having the essence of God, i.e., the knowable reality of God. That is, it depends on the collapse into one of Plotinus' "One" and "Mind"; see Axel Dahl, *Augustin und Plotin* (Lund, 1945), pp. 34–43. That is, it depends on Augustine's rejection of Plotinus' doctrine that God is the One-above-Being, in favor of a doctrine that God is Being-as-such. What happened is that Augustine *both* achieved an anti-Plotinian identification of God as Being-itself, in which the differentiations of the Plotinian divine hierarchy are collapsed, and yet continued to apprehend God's *triune* character on the model of that hierarchy. The combination was the disaster.

69. Peter Lombard *Sentences* 1.32.3. See also Bonaventure *Sentences* 32.1.1; 32.2.1–2; Aquinas *Summa* 1.31.39.

70. On the technical history of medieval trinitarianism, see A. Michel, "Trinité," *DThC* 15/2:1698–1764; "Relations Divines," ibid., 13/2: 2135–56.

71. E.g., Augustine *Letters* 170.3–6; *Trinity* 8.1.

72. Lombard *Sentences* 1.19.4.

73. Ibid., 1.19.5. In Augustine, e.g., *Trinity* 6.12. This is the doctrine termed "perichoresis."

74. Augustine *Letters* 120.17.

75. Augustine *Trinity* 8.1.

76. Council of Florence, "Decree for the Copts," in *Conciliorum Oecumenicorum Decreta*, pp. 57–58.

77. Lombard *Sentences* 1.19.4–14.

78. Aquinas *Summa* 1.28.2.

79. E.g., ibid., 1.27; Bonaventure *Sentences* 13.1. That this is Au-

gustine's doctrine, see Michael Schmaus, *Die Psychologische Trinita-etslehre des heiligen Augustinus* (Münster, 1927), pp. 127–36.

80. E.g., Aquinas *Summa* 1.27.1.

81. E.g., ibid., 1.28.1. This is again Augustine's doctrine; *Trinity* 5.3–6.

82. In these formalities I will follow Aquinas' form of teaching. Here, *Summa* 1.28.4.

83. Ibid., 1.32.3.

84. Ibid., 1.40.4.

85. This is the main line, from Lombard to Aquinas and to Alexander of Hales and Bonaventure. It was denied by a line of thinkers from Gilbert de la Porée to Durand of Saint-Pourcain. See Michel, "Trinité," cols. 1615–1732; "Relations," cols. 2145ff.

86. E.g., Bonaventure *Sentences* 23.1.1–2; 25.1.1–2.

87. Aquinas *Summa* 1.29.4. In general see Michel, "Trinité": col. 1736 re Bonaventure; cols. 1742–43 re Aquinas.

88. Lombard *Sentences* 1.26.2–3.

89. As did Gilbert de la Porée; see Michel, "Trinité," cols. 1715–29.

90. Lombard *Sentences* 1.5.

91. Lateran Council, session 4, constitution 2 in *Conciliorum Oecumenicorum Decreta*, pp. 231–33.

92. Augustine *Trinity* 1.3.

93. Ibid., 6.17. See Schindler, *Wort*, p. 162.

94. Aquinas *Summa* 1.43.2. Lombard *Sentences* 1.14–16; 1.14.1; Bonaventure *Sentences* 15.1.2.

95. Augustine *Trinity* 4.28.

96. Aquinas *Summa* 1.27.5

97. The incompatibility of this system with trinitarian faith is clearly shown by Augustine's hopeless problem with the Spirit, always the key identity in trinitarian reflection. See, e.g., *Trinity* 5.16; to salvage the hypostasis of the Spirit and the biblical language, Augustine must violate his system. He cannot abide that the Spirit's being given to creatures could be the relation which is the Spirit's inner-divine reality, but the best he can do is found the Spirit's prior reality in the predestination of some creatures to receive the Spirit— which is not better but worse for him, introducing potentiality into God. The most charitable thing that can be said of all this is that in the conflict between Augustine's faith and his theology, he on this point goes with his faith. It would have been better, of course, also to change the theology.

98. Augustine *Trinity* 6.12.

99. Ibid., 5.10; 7.7–11.

100. Lombard *Sentences* 1.13.

101. Michel, "Trinité," cols. 1731–53.

102. Basil the Great *On the Holy Spirit (PG* 32:37–38*)*. Or see Athanasius *Letter to Serapion IV.*

103. Augustine *John* 20.3; *Trinity* 1.12.15; *Handbook on Faith Hope and Charity* 38 (*CChr.SL* 46 [1969]; 49–114).

104. Augustine *Trinity* 4.30.

105. Ibid., 1.7–10.

106. Ibid., 2; 3.3.

107. Lombard *Sentences* 3.1.3. Bonaventure's discussion shows especially bluntly how totally the hermeneutic function of "Father"/"Son"/"Spirit" has been lost; e.g., *Sentences* 3.1.1.4. He lays down the basic proposition that "the Father or the Spirit can . . . form a . . . human body . . . and join this to himself." And to the argument that then the first or third person would be "Son of God" on earth, and the second person "Son of God" in the Trinity, he blandly asks, "Why not?"

108. Schindler, *Wort,* p. 167; Dahl, *Augustin,* p. 12.

109. See Schindler, *Wort,* e.g., p. 180. I must say a word to recent and current controversy about the function of Augustine's soul analogies. Schindler is right that Augustine is not out to create a "psychological Trinity-doctrine," as Schmaus supposed. The analogies do not explicate God's triunity, and Augustine knows they do not. But neither is it the human soul that Augustine chiefly wishes to explicate, as Schindler thinks. The analogies are indeed not intended to explain the Trinity, but they are intended to give meaning to our language about the Trinity. In general, the distinction between truth and meaning is ignored in this particular debate.

110. Augustine states the argument of the whole *On the Trinity* at 15.1.

111. Ibid., 1.2–9; Lombard *Sentences* 1.15–16. See Maier, *Missions.*

112. Augustine *Trinity* 4.28.

113. Ibid., 4.29.

114. Ibid., 1.19.

115. Ibid., 1.18; 15.31–37.

116. Ibid., 15.7

117. Michel, "Trinité," cols. 177–79. E.g., in Augustine *Trinity* 1.19.

118. Augustine *Trinity*, 1.8.
119. Maier, *Missions*, pp. 154–56.
120. Augustine *Trinity* 4.28.
121. Maier, *Missions*, pp. 168–75.
122. E.g., Bonaventure *Sentences* 9.10.
123. See above all du Roy, *L'intelligence*, esp. pp. 420–28, 447–50. In Augustine's *On the Trinity*, it is the pivotal argument of 8 that makes this move; but see also such blunt statements as those of 11.11.18.
124. Du Roy, *L'intelligence*, pp. 447ff.
125. Ibid., p. 447.
126. Augustine *City* 9.26.7–9.
127. E.g., Augustine *Trinity* 8.3–6, 9–15.
128. Ibid., 14.12.
129. Pervasive in *City of God*.
130. Augustine *Trinity* 8; 9.1–3.
131. Ibid., 9.3–4.
132. Ibid., 10.
133. Summarizing, ibid., 4.23.
134. Also the special attributions of memory to the Father, knowledge to the Son, and love to the Spirit are at the end attacked by the same old anti-Cappadocian scruples; *Trinity* 15.12.28. So that we end with the same ontologically weak analogies, "appropriations," as those from the visible missions; ibid., 15.12.29–32. Thus Augustine must after all explicitly deny that the consciousness analogies give any meaning to the assertion of the *three* in God—which after all is the whole difficulty; ibid., 15.12.23.
135. Maier, *Missions*, p. 187.
136. If we line up his main soul analyses in columns, so,

being	knowledge	will
lover	loved	love
mind	knowledge	love
memory	knowledge	will

the asserted equivalence of the terms in the first column gives this proposition: the being of mind as subject is immediate self-consciousness. And there is future Western philosophy in a nutshell.
137. Augustine *Trinity* 15.10.
138. E.g., du Roy, *L'intelligence*, p. 462.
139. The extreme of this is reached in standard seventeenth- and eighteenth-century Calvinism, i.e., in the theology which has most

shaped the American church. See, e.g., the textbook for colonial and federal theological instruction, William Ames' *The Marrow of Theology* (1623).

140. The observation is by no means original with me. Notably, it was made by Friedrich Schleiermacher, *The Christian Faith*, cited here from the 7th edition (Berlin: de Gruyter, 1960), pp. 458–73.

141. Emanuel Hirsch, *Geschichte der neuern evanglischen Theologie* (Gütersloh: Bertelsmann, 1951), 2:114–20, 186–93.

142. John Locke, *The Reasonableness of Christianity as Delivered in the Scriptures* (1695).

143. H. Bornkamm, "Servet," *RGG*³ 5:1714; H. R. Guggisberg, "Sozinianer," *RGG*³ 6:207–10; M. Schmidt, "Unitarier," *RGG*³ 6:1148–51.

144. Hirsch, *Geschichte*, 4:1–119.

145. Such critique has not abated in our century. Currently influential are the arguments of Cyril Richardson, *The Doctrine of the Trinity* (New York: Abingdon, 1958), that inherited trinitarianism is the result of the use of inappropriate biblical and Hellenic language to state necessary theological insight into God's "transcendence" and "immanence"; of G. W. H. Lampe, *God as Spirit* (Oxford: Clarendon, 1977), that we need more "personal" language and that the metaphysical problems generated by traditional language are insoluble; and of C. F. D. Moule, *The Holy Spirit* (Oxford: Mowbray, 1978), pp. 43–51, that a binity would make sense but that there is no need to make a "person" of the Spirit. In general, such critiques are not very different from those of the previous two centuries, and somewhat less impressive. In some ways, Richardson's critique of the tradition parallels that of this book in that it is directed against the Logos theology of the Apologists. But he fails to see that the classic doctrine is itself the result of just such critique. In other ways, his argument depends on uncritical assumption of just those metaphysical axioms against which trinitarianism is directed. Lampe's book is a classic case of the kind of omnivorous scholarship that knows everything and understands little, and ends by certifying the received wisdom of the scholar's own education. As for Moule, the great biblical teacher's arguments all suppose the common account, that the affirmation of the Spirit's *hypostasia* was a mere imitation of the Son's confirmation in that status. As we have seen, it did not work so.

146. The classical document of Enlightenment religion is Immanuel Kant, *Religion Within the Bounds of Reason Alone* (1783). For a splendid analysis, see Hirsch, *Geschichte*, 4:271–76, 320–29.

147. Schleiermacher, *Christian Faith*, 170.1.

148. Ibid., 170.3.

149. Ibid., 171.2–5.

150. Ibid., 171.52.

151. Ibid., 171.1.

152. Friedrich Schleiermacher, *A Brief Outline of Theological Study*, 43–53; *Christian Faith*, 171.3–6.

153. *Christian Faith*, 172.3.

154. Georg F. W. Hegel, *Phenomenology of Spirit* 4A, 7C; *Lectures on the Philosophy of Religion*, intro., parts 1, 3. See Robert W. Jenson, *God after God* (Indianapolis: Bobbs-Merrill, 1969), pp. 33–35.

155. John Macquarrie, *Principles of Christian Theology* (New York: Scribner's, 1966), pp. 94–110, 174–93; Paul Tillich, *Systematic Theology* (Chicago: University of Chicago Press, 1963), 3:283–94.

156. To Barth's trinitarianism, Eberhard Jüngel, *The Doctrine of the Trinity* (Grand Rapids: Eerdmans, 1976); and now Colin Gunton, *Becoming and Being* (Oxford: Oxford University Press, 1978), pp. 117–85.

157. See Jenson, *God*, pp. 95–156.

158. Karl Barth, *Kirchliche Dogmatik* (Zurich: Zollikon, 1932–67), 1/1:32, 329.

159. Ibid., pp. 319, 331, 352.

160. Ibid., pp. 311–16.

161. Ibid., p. 312.

162. Ibid., pp. 321–22.

163. To this and the rest of the paragraph, Jenson, *God*, pp. 101–8.

164. Ibid., p. 404.

165. Robert W. Jenson, *Alpha and Omega* (New York: Nelson, 1963), pp. 72–83.

166. Karl Barth, *Dogmatik*, 1/1:369.

167. Ibid., pp. 370ff.

168. Ibid., pp. 373ff.

169. Ibid., p. 369.

170. Ibid., pp. 369ff.

171. Cf. Jenson, *God*, pp. 139–56.

172. This is also the place to commend to readers other current trinitarian thinkers whom I can regard as allies in the immediate task. I mention Karl Rahner, *The Trinity*, trans. J. Donceel (New York: Herder, 1970); Jüngel, *Trinity*; D. M. MacKinnon, "The Relation of the Doctrines of the Incarnation and the Trinity," in *Creation, Christ, and Culture*, Festschrift for T. R. Torrance, ed. R. W. A. McKinney (Edinburgh: T. & T. Clark, 1976), pp. 92–107.

173. Eberhard Jüngel, "Das Verhältnis von 'ökonomisches' and 'immaneter' Trinität," *ZThK* 72 (1975): 353–65; p. 363: "The concept of the divine essence can no longer be thought in abstraction from the event of God's triune existence." Peter Brunner, "Die Freiheit des Menschen in Gottes Heilsgeschichte," in *Pro Ecclesia* (Berlin: Lutherisches Verlaghaus, 1962), 1:110: "In view of God's . . . self-determination to us, we must and may abandon all pictures of God, that with the use of antiquity's modes of thought read a fixed, un-moveable and abstract unchangeability into God . . . , so that . . . all talk about new judgments, new reactions, new deeds and words in God . . . must appear as naive anthropomorphisms." The demand for overcoming the timelessness axiom is endemic in twentieth-century theology. Attempts actually to do so are those of Karl Barth on the one hand and "process theology" on the other. On the great difference between the two and in conclusive refutation of the second, see Gunton, *Becoming*.

174. See Carl Heinz Ratschow, *Lutherische Dogmatik Zwischen Reformation und Aufklärung* (Gütersloh: Mohn, 1964–), part 2.

175. E.g., Johann Friedrich König, *Theologia positiva acroamatica* (1664), pp. 142–57.

176. Rahner, *Trinity*, pp. 21–22; Jüngel, "Verhaltnis."

177. Athanasius *Serapion IV* 3.

178. E.g., again, Augustine *Trinity* 4.3.

179. Bluntly, Tertullian *Against Praxeas* 9.2–3.

180. Basil the Great *Holy Spirit* 47; Bonaventure *Sentences* 7.a.1., p. ii.

181. M. Douglas Meeks, "Gott und die Ökonomia des Heiligen Geistes," *EvTh* 40 (1980): 40–58, analyzing the connection of asymmetric trinitarianism and economic bondage.

182. Franz K. Mayr, "Trinitätstheologie und theologische Anthropologie," *ZThK* 68 (1971): 427–77.

183. Augustine *Trinity* 9–14 produces a series of soul images of the Trinity. Their sequence is essential. He begins with lover/loved/love (9.2). But it is axiomatic for Augustine that to make the imaging work we must select that form of love in which the lover has no other object than himself (9.3). It is only the soul as self-contained substance, not the soul in relation, that can be an analog of Augustine's God. Inside the substance-soul, the love triplet is mind/knowledge/love (9.3–4), and this again, burrowing yet deeper into a self-contained dialectic, is memory/intelligence/will (10). See Schindler, *Wort*, pp. 177–80. Nor does Hegel truly break out from the position. It is

in knowing the world, not in knowing Jesus, that Hegel's God has himself as Object; the creation of the world and the begetting of the Son are, while distinguishable as idea from *Vorstellung,* only one event. But in that the world is a universal and not a particular, God is not by this knowledge involved intersubjectively; he remains finally at rest in his own encompassing being.

184. Du Roy, *L'intelligence,* p. 464.

185. Peter Brunner, unpublished Heidelberg lectures, Autumn 1954.

186. Ibid.

5

Triune Infinity

Throughout I have insisted on the clash of the gospel's and Hellenism's interpretations of God and have blamed Western theology's trinitarian enfeeblement on defeat in this battle. It is time to reiterate that I do not intend thereby to decry the "Hellenization" of Christianity or to propose termination of the metaphysical reflection in which the confrontation with Hellenism has involved the gospel. On the contrary, the fault of Western trinitarianism was precisely a failure to carry on the metaphysical creativity begun by the Cappadocians, and so long as the Western church endures, it must be Hellenic. Returns to the "simple gospel" seldom land at their intended destination; they land instead at whatever interpretation of reality is currently most hallowed by familiarity, however it may be related to the gospel. So at least it went with Augustine's rejection of Cappadocian subtleties, and so it would surely go with any trinitarian primitivism of ours.

Therefore I must conclude this book by proceeding to some beginnings of that revisionist metaphysics, the necessity of which I have several times asserted. God—trinitarian identification of God compelled us to say—is an event, and one, we may now add, constituted in relations and personal in structure. Our question must be: What sense can it make to call God an event? To say that an event "upholds the universe" or "speaks through the prophets"? Any properly formed sentence can of course be made to make sense by reinterpretation of "sense," that is, by revision of our grasp of reality. So our question becomes: how must reality be interpreted, if its God is triune? If he is the event between Father, Son, and Spirit?

161

We will launch our reflection by considering the one as yet undiscussed aspect of Gregory of Nyssa's trinitarian reflection: his doctrine of divine infinity. Thus we will both complete our picture of trinitarian history's great era and pick up the enterprise of constructive trinitarian metaphysics where its central task was dropped. Readers familiar with Gregory's text will perhaps judge that at some place in the next section they have stopped hearing Gregory and hear only the present author. Perhaps they will draw the line where the notes stop; I will not be greatly alarmed wherever they draw it.

Infinite Deity

By Hellenic, and so by ordinary Christian interpretation, God not only has but is an *ousia*. As noted before, an *ousia* is *what is* something-or-other, by possession of a definite complex of attributes specifying "some-," or *ousia* is what is thus possessed. And the word in speculative use hovers between the two senses. It is from the play between the two that speculative use of *ousia* has its existential meaning. As substantial, I *have* the characteristics of vertebrateness, linguisticality, and so on; and what I *am is* the complex of these characteristics; and having and being thus each depends on and necessitates the other. Insofar as I am substantial, I am a possessor and maintain myself in being by what I possess.

In standard Christian metaphysics, God too is a substance; indeed, he is the only true substance, so that with him we may drop the above "insofar." That is, God is the possessor of some definite complex of attributes and maintains himself eternally in being by the utter security of his grasp upon them. Just so, of course, he *must* hang onto them.

As we have seen, Cappadocian trinitarianism broke up this conceptuality. By distinguishing *ousia* from *hypostasis* in the case of God, Basil and his protégés pushed God's *ousia* unambiguously to the side of the possessed complex of attributes. Their possessor would now have to be either the event of which the Cappadocians predicate "God," or the hypostases, singly or together. The play of possessor and possessed, which animates Hellenic metaphysics, is thus dissolved; God only *has* an *ousia;* he *is* not one. And then Gregory of Nyssa denied that God's *ousia* could be any list of linked attributes which God must always continue to exemplify in order to be God. The biblical God cannot be thus bounded, constrained by what already was and is true of him. But what then can *ousia* mean?

The ordinary assertion of God's ineffability has not gone as far as Gregory's. We may refrain from asserting that any particular characteristic is binding upon God, and so say that we "cannot know God's being," that we cannot know what he necessarily permanently is, and yet use the word "God" in the same way we use apparently similar terms (e.g., "the Emperor") of entities of which we do possess such knowledge. That is, we may use "God" as what Gregory called a "name that denotes the nature and is more than a metaphor,"[1] even if we allow that this nature is permanently obscure to us. By our language we thus posit that there *is* a complex of essential divine attributes even though we cannot know what they are. We suppose that God knows marks he must always manifest to be God, even if we cannot.[2] Far more radically, Gregory claims that divine being, at least, is no such definite complex of characteristics at all. He denies that God has any "name that denotes the nature and is more than a metaphor." Divine being is "infinite,"[3] the very absence of restraint by what is already the case, even about the being that is infinite.

Infinite being is an odd sort of being. It cannot be anything other than its infinity, cannot be an infinite something, for there can be no infinite *some*-thing: A substance without clear boundaries could be only a wavery, insubstantial substance, and a substance with no boundaries must instantly dissipate. Just this observation was the starting point of Hellenic philosophy's analysis of the notion of infinity. An infinite something would always generate new characteristics beyond those that make its given self at any moment. Thus Aristotle: "That is infinite . . . which has always something beyond itself."[4] Therefore an infinite something would have no "nature" at all, for a "nature" is precisely what *defines*, that is, limits, the possibilities of an entity.[5] Just so, an entity's nature subjects it to knowledge.[6] The syllogistic proof "All humans are mortal. Socrates is a human. Therefore Socrates is mortal" transforms the true guess that Socrates is mortal into actual knowledge, but it can do so only because humanity names a fixed and finite set of characteristics.[7] Did it not, the minor premise would instantly transform itself into a whole new syllogism, with its own minor premise, which would do the same and so on; and the security of knowledge, as over against guessing, would never be achieved. On both these counts, God—in the judgment of Hellenic philosophy—cannot be infinite; this is the one negative predicate that cannot fit deity, for it is deity's function to be the final object of knowledge, the middle term of the proof of the world's existence. And the very difference of God and world, of timelessness and time, presumes that God is *not* the world and is *not* temporal, that is, that there are limits to what deity is and can be.[8]

The Christian attribution of infinity to God is thus in itself a radical reversal of metaphysical values. And more in the direct line of our present argument, if God's being is infinite, then divine being is nothing other than infinity as such. What the three divine hypostases variously derive from each other, so as to be distinguishably three and so that their joint act can be called "God," is sheer unboundedness.

Of course, if talk of "infinity" is to have any sense at all, infinity must surely be the infinity *of* something. And Gregory's analysis does say what is infinite, but this is not a set of essentially divine attributes or their possessor, to make a referent for "deity" in the usual style. In Gregory's interpretation, there *is*, most strictly speaking, no *some*-thing, God. If believing in God means being a "theist," Gregory is an atheist—which is what pagan Hellenists regularly took the Christians to be. The divine *ousia* is the infinity—and this is its sole characterization—of the work done between Jesus and his Father in their Spirit. That what these three do is *God*, that they "have divine being," means sheerly that what happens among them accepts no limits, that nothing can hinder the life and love they enact—that the Father's choice will embrace all events, Jesus' self-giving outlast all unbelief, the Future they send be inexhaustible.

As my language has already been driven by the logic of the case to show, the infinity that is, according to Gregory, God's *ousia*, is *temporal* infinity.[9] God is not infinite because he time- lessly *extends* to all reality, but because time cannot exhaust or keep up with his activity: "The transcendent and blessed Life has neither interior measure nor compass, for no temporal ex- tension can keep pace with it."[10] In the Hellenic tradition, that something was "infinite" meant that it *lacks* definition. Greg- ory's God, on the contrary, is infinite in that he *overcomes* all definitions, in that he has irresistible Possibility: "The un- created nature differs greatly from the created. That is limited; this has no limits. That is bounded by appropriate . . . mea- sures; this is measured only by limitlessness . . . [and so] evades every quantitative concept, by which one could bring the mind to bear. . . . In created life we can find a beginning and an end; but the Blessedness beyond creation accepts nei- ther beginning nor end."[11]

Hellenic deity is eternal in that in it circling time has its motionless center: Gregory's God is eternal in that he envelops time, is ahead of and so before it.[12] The Greek's God stands still, so that we may ground moving things in him; Gregory's God keeps things moving.[13] And Gregory is clear about the contrast; he mocks the Arians for ranking the Logos, who "works the deeds of philanthropy," below their "Unbegotten," whose Hellenic perfection merely makes him in Gregory's view "inactive."[14]

Moreover, as Gregory's language of life and motion already shows, it is by time's proper reality as futurity that he interprets God's infinity. Explicitly, "the identifying mark of the divine life . . . is that always God must be said to be: 'He was not . . . ' or 'He will not be . . . ' never fit him. . . . We teach . . . what we have heard from the prophets . . . , that he is king before all ages and will rule through all ages . . . , that he is infinite over against the past and over against the future. . . . So we must ask [the

Arians] why they define God's being by its having no beginning and not by its having no end. . . . Indeed, if they must divide eternity, let them reverse their doctrine and reckon endless futurity the mark of deity . . . , finding their axioms in what is to come and is real in hope, rather than in what is past and old."[15] Note also that Gregory does *not* say, as Augustine: "'He was' or 'He will be' never fit God."

To be God is, in this interpretation, always to have future. The action that is God, is *God*, "has divine being," just in that it transcends all past-imposed conditions. To claim, for instance, that Jesus has the divine being, and to say, "In his name, I forgive your sins," thereby claiming that his love unconditionally, eschatologically, transcends guilt, are equivalent. And "behind" or "above" the unconditioned happening with Jesus and his Father and their Spirit, there is no-thing, only the illimitable Possibility which the event opens before himself. "Divine being," as used by Gregory, is the Cheshire-cat grin of Hellenic *ousia*-deity, made to be merely a means of attributing infinity to something else, the work of Father, Son, and Spirit. As we have seen, even the lingering grin will be a temptation to later theology, but that is not our concern at present.

The "one divine *ousia*," the *varied* sharing of which distinguishes Father, Son, and Spirit, and the varied *sharing* of which qualifies their joint act as God, is *temporal unhinderedness*, the fact that the act of Father, Son, and Spirit overcomes all conditions. Whether the temporal conditions on what happens with Christ are the blunders of the past, of our guilt and codified errors, or the dismally random predictabilities of the future, or the established immobilities of the present, they are overcome in the divine action, which just in this overcoming— as it must then draw *all* things finally *together*—is one *divine* action and *one* divine action. That time cannot overhaul him is what Jesus receives from his relation to the Father. Just so, the Spirit that "goes out" from them is the very Power of futurity.

The three identities are identities of *one* God, by the structure of that same transcendence in which they are identities of *God*.

Jesus' love is the love of God in that it is in all ways final. And there can be only one final event. It is in that Jesus' love will be the outcome of time's sequences that it is also their beginning; and what now happens is precisely the opening of what already is to what may come of it, that is, the occurrence of possibility. The structure of transcendence, in which the three identities are the repeated identity of one God, is not the persistence of an *ousia* nature; it is the freedom of the future to overcome all persistence, and just so to fulfill all that otherwise would merely have persisted. It is Spirit.

Thus each identity has its priority. The Son is epistemologically prior. The Father has the ontic priority; he is the given transcendence to Jesus, and the given of hope and love. But the Spirit has the metaphysical priority; the only definition of God in Scripture is that "God is Spirit" (John 4:24). It is this structure of priorities that is the "substantiality" of God.

To be God is to be Father, Son, and Spirit, as each identity is both other than and of the same God as the other two, in and by the structure of relations just described. To be God, therefore, is to be freedom from oneself as given, yet for oneself as given. To be God is to be the power of the future to transcend what is, precisely insofar as God is himself responsible for what is, and just so to fulfill what is. To be God is to be the one for whom Second Isaiah could say, "Forget the former things. See, I will do a new thing" (Isa. 43:18–19), where the former things were his own past acts as God, and who would, by doing the new thing, prove that the very doer of the old things was indeed God. To be God is to possess oneself only as the opportunity of being other than the possessed self. To be God is to be the Eschatos.

A last step: What all these dialectics are denotatively about is the resurrection of Jesus. If indeed Jesus the Israelite, this particular man, specified by his particular heritage and story, died and yet lives, then these dialectics touch reality. If not, they do not touch reality. It is if Jesus is risen that there is an unconditional lover with the limit of love behind him. It is if there is such a lover that the human enterprise has the sort of conclusion theology calls Eschaton, a fulfillment of what has occupied time that just so is freedom from what has occupied time, an end that is at once outcome and beginning, conclusion and overcoming.

To say that these "ifs" are fulfilled, that it *is* so, is to say that reality is very different from what we would otherwise have expected. It is when we try explicitly to display this oddity that we speak of what the gospel calls "God." If the claims about Jesus are true, time is odd over against our expectations of it. It is this oddity about time that is God.

As all the ontological determinants of the God of classical Western culture-religion came together in his *ousia,* so those of the gospel's God come together in the event of Jesus' resurrection. If Jesus is not risen, this God simply is not. If we bend the old language a little, instead of replacing it, we may say that the resurrection is this God's *ousia.*

Triune Infinity

Sheer Possibility, which the argument of the previous section has opened before all reality, is not my invention; it is none other than that stark Transcendence which has been the challenge and curse of Western life. From the gospel, we have learned that anything can be. If we believe both the gospel and this its metaphysical lesson, we are freed to unstoppable creativity, to the role and status of pioneers of being. But if we retain only the lesson and forget the gospel, we are freed to mere metaphysical vertigo, to an uncontrolled and endless flight through temporal space: "What did we do, when we tore the earth from its sun . . . ? Whither do we now move? Away from *all* suns? Do we not plunge endlessly? And lurch backward, sideward, forward? Is there any above and below more? Do we not wander through an endless nothingness?"[16]

If temporal reality is bracketed by the specific eternity of the triune God, it is bracketed by the specific deity of this God, by unbounded futurity. If the gospel, which asserts this God, is *true,* then this futurity is really there, and we must expect that when the gospel calls our attention to it, it will be noticed also by those of us who do not come to obey the gospel.[17] To such notice, unbounded futurity must present itself as the child's nightmare of eternity, in which at every moment there is always yet another moment, so that no journey can have a goal, no pain a termination, no joy a resting place, into which the meaning of every temporal act and sequence evaporates.

If infinity is not the infinity of God, it must be the infinity of the world, that is, nothingness. The one who hears the call of infinity must believe either in Christ or in nothing. Insofar as the call of infinity has been an actual historical phenomenon in the West, and insofar as we have variously heard it, radical faith and nihilism have repeatedly and with increasing urgency posited themselves as our only choices;[18] we need affirm the systems of neither Søren Kierkegaard nor Jean-Paul Sartre to see that each of us must in a deep sense be the one or the other.

It is at least abstractly possible that the nightmare of the unobeyed gospel is true, that the preaching of the gospel in the West has revealed our true metaphysical case even though the gospel itself is false. Then the sundry nihilisms that flourish in secularized Western history—from bureaucratic capitalism to self-development religions—are right, are in accord with reality. If, on the other hand, the gospel is itself true, then the unbounded futurity that goes before us is not mere endlessness. But then what is it? How does unbounded futurity present itself to *believing* notice?

To grasp temporal infinity in a way appropriate to the gospel and so as the real basis not of nihilism but of unquenchable hope, that is, to grasp temporal infinity as it in fact must be if the gospel is true, we must do something the Cappadocians did not. We must consider this divine *ousia* not merely as its posit enables us to interpret the Trinity, but also as, conversely, the character of infinity and time is determined by the fact of divine triunity. That is, we must adumbrate a trinitarian concept of infinite futurity.

It is specifically as the Spirit that God comes to us from the unsurpassable future, that he is the Power of the Eschaton. Divine temporal infinity is thus the ascendancy of this coming; it is the unconditionality of the gospel's promises, the certainty of sacramental presence to believers and unbelievers alike, the beauty and implausibility and inevitability of believers' political and social visions, the uncompromised forgiveness of sin.

Throughout the church's history, two experiences of spirit have struggled to interpret the Spirit. The one is of unidentifiable dynamism that simply seizes us for the future—any future, whatever future is on its way—and just, and only apparently paradoxically, so is immediately self-authenticating in experience. It is to this experience that "enthusiastic" movements in Christianity, from Montanism to congregational "human potential" groups, have covertly appealed—covertly because overt appeal means departing from christological confession. It is the same experience which in secularized form is the empty freedom of existentialism and of the debased American slogan "It's a free country." The other experience has a very different phenomenal structure; spirit is here always the spirit-of someone, Lincoln's spirit or the spirit of '76 or the team's spirit. When this structure is allowed to rule our interpretation of the Spirit, as it must if we are to agree with Scripture, the Spirit is always specifically Jesus' spirit and the Father's.

The temporal infinity ahead of all things does not merely stretch forward on and on. Temporal infinity is spirit, of the proper second sort just described, spirit-*of* someone. Thus temporal infinity has specific character, which is the matter of the next paragraphs. And it has the recursive shape marked by "of," the object of which preposition is necessarily somehow given *before* ultimate futurity. A great deal has been made of the contrast between the Bible's "linear" interpretation of time[19] and the "circular" repetition of mythic time, and I too have insisted on it. But if we simply extrapolate from these interpretations to concepts of eternity, we obtain eternity either as time that goes on forever or eternity as the still point at the center of circling time. Neither will do for the gospel. Triune infinity does not bracket time by going on forever in both directions from it. Eternity as the Spirit is rather the inexhaustibility of the relation between Jesus as the final Lord and all that precedes his coming. That is, true temporal infinity is the inexhaustibility of the transformation of all temporal events in and as the last event, "after" which there are indeed no others. This transformation is the transformation that love is, which brings us to the Son.

The infinite Spirit is the Spirit of Jesus. Thus divine temporal infinity is, second, the inexhaustibility of the life lived by Jesus. Jesus' life, to be that of a particular individual, is bounded. Like that of every created person, it is defined by its sequence of events, its plot, as this sequence is made into a determinate whole, into a possibly plotted sequence, by his particular death. By the events of Jesus' life, in their actual sequence, and by his particular death, this specific human happens to be defined as the man for others, as a life not merely in fact given for his sisters and brothers but determined as a whole by that giving. He *is* the crucified, whose life was lived for and by the promise he had to proclaim to others, whom the evangelist John could call the Sent One (e.g., John 3:23–36), and who finally gave up himself wholly to that promise.

Thus, that the Eschaton will be the triumph of this *defined* individual is not contrary to the posit of *infinite* futurity; it is constitutive thereof. For the Eschaton is the triumph of an individual whose very individuality is that he does not and need not cling to what *he* is or has, whose very individuality is his unhindered way to others, is his freedom from his merely individual self. In the final community constituted by *his* presence, there will be no end to mutual possibility—and that is the infinity of the biblical God.

With these analyses and with those just made about the Spirit, we are in the midst of the antinomy that agitates every eschatology. The promise of an Outcome must promise *something*, must call forward to a specifiable, describable state of affairs. If I call you merely to *an* outcome, you cannot know whether this is a promise or a threat, and so it can be neither. To make a promise I must say, "Thus and such will come to pass." But then it becomes doubtful that any eschatological promise can be meaningful, for if an eschatological promise is of a definite state of affairs, when that state arrives, what then? Does it merely persist timelessly? Then true human being is

after all escape from time—and I should not now live by promises, including this one! Is it succeeded by other states? Then
it is not the eschaton.

The antinomy is not esoteric or my arbitrary dialectical invention. It is the very problem that drove Rudolf Bultmann to
attempt a contentless eschatology, to hope only to be able to
keep on hoping.[20] It disturbs the various futurist movements
in contemporary theology.[21] And it was the dialectical engine
of the secularization that has opened the West to a nihilist
eschatology, to a vision of empty boundless futurity. The antinomy is solved in one case only: when what is eschatologically promised is *love,* the specific love which in historic fact is
enacted by Jesus.

Love is a possible described state of events. I can very well
say I hope to love and be loved and say it in such a way that
certain events will fulfill my hope and other certain events disappoint it. If some day I must judge that the waiting has been
too long and that Jesus' love will not triumph, I will be able to
tell how my hope is disappointed. And love is always particular: To love and be loved by Henry is one thing, to love and
be loved by William another, and one can specify the difference. The love which the gospel eschatogically promises is
Jesus' love, the love defined by his life and death; if some day
the Hidden Imam in fact appears as judge of the living and the
dead, Christians will be able to tell that our hope has been
disappointed.

But when love comes, life neither thereby becomes un-
eventful nor needs to move on from love to remain eventful,
for to love someone is precisely to affirm his or her freedom,
his or her unfettered novelty over against me; it is to occupy
a space of freedom that encompasses us both. To love someone
is to say, "I now know my own good only by reference to you:
I will not bind in advance what you will do with and for me,
only choose that whatever you do will be my good." When
love happens, eventful futurity, creation, and surprise only
begin.

Thus the coming of love is an event that can occur and not
be followed—forever, if the love is unconditional—without

thereby again locating value in what has come to pass and endures, without constituting a *finished* reality, without abolishing promise. For love is very openness to an unbounded possibility of surprise, to the making and hearing and fulfilling of promise.

It is love that is eschatologically promised. The infinite futurity that encompasses all things is the space of utter freedom that Jesus and we will occupy in that our community will be constituted by his crucified and risen and therefore unconditional love.

Compelled to use "love" to explicate reality's infinite futurity, I am, third, compelled to think this infinity as personal. Thus I come to the Father, for when we think God as person we posit the Father, in that we think God as knowing and willing himself in the Son and having the unity of his knowing and willing in the Spirit as Love. The Father *intends* himself in the Son and intends all creatures by the way he intends the Son. Divine infinity is the infinity of this intension; that is, it is the infinity of a specific—loving—*consciousness*.

Consciousness is, as has often been noted, in itself infinite. Every cognition and every act of will leads on to further cognitions and volitions. Just so, consciousness has never successfully been interpreted as substance,[22] for considered *in itself*, as substances must be, consciousness has no center, fleeing from itself in all temporal directions. Consciousness has a center only in that it is in fact not in itself, only in that it is essentially given an *object*, an opaque resistance to its flight toward universal clarity, a self-renewing occasion of puzzlement and difficulty, that responds to every cognitive success with a new problem produced by the success itself, and to every purposeful use with a new moral challenge. Only as thus reflected back from objects is consciousness centered, so that there *is* consciousness and can be such an entity as *a* consciousness. And only in that some of these objects are—objectively!— other subjects is a consciousness *self*-consciousness, to be a continuing entity, though of a very different sort than are "substances." Just so, it appears that an actual consciousness must—to be at all—be frustrated in an intrinsic infinity; parodying Sartre,[23] a consciousness is that which must try to be infinite and fail.

An actually infinite consciousness could only be one that encountered a genuine, resistant object, and so was centered, without thereby being impeded in his intension of other objects beyond and yet others beyond those and. . . . Just this is asserted of the Father and his Son. Jesus is a creature, an other than mere God. And in Jesus' personal identification with sinful humanity, he is an actual *problem* for his Father, for at the end of all subtleties, sin and all evil can only be specified as that which God does not want.[24] But in that this Jesus is just in this very identification the creature for all others, the one whose individuality consists in surrender of all individual claims, the Father's preoccupation with him, Jesus' objectopacity to the Father's outward flight of pure knowledge and will, does not impede the way of the Father's intension to all things; it *is* the way.

The world, then, has infinity before it in that it is intended by an infinite consciousness. The great metaphysical claim of the gospel is that the freedom in which all events occur is neither deaf nor dumb, to say nothing of blind. It speaks, and more to our present point, it can be *addressed*. The great metaphysical issue between the believing and nihilist forms of infinite expectation is whether petitionary prayer is a reasonable enterprise or not, whether the freedom in which all events occur, if futurity is infinite, is consciousness or accident.

In the course of the history of Western unbelief, we have come sometimes to experience the infinite future as the field of pure chance, as the essentially endless remaining segment of the crap game that reality plays. And we have come sometimes to experience the infinite future as the endless unrolling of a course of events determined at every moment by what precedes it. It is worth noting that these apparently opposite interpretations turn out on reflection to be logically and experientially indistinguishable. The alternative to Western nihilism is the gospel's claim that all events happen in freedom—a claim which does not, we should note, conflict at all with commonsensical or scientific prediction—*and* that this freedom can be appealed to.

We must quickly move to avert a mythological misunderstanding of these last assertions. Thinking of the Father as consciousness intending the Son and the world, we may slide into thinking of the Father as a supernatural person—in the modern sense of "person"—out there looking at us. But a consciousness, which the Father is in his identity-distinction from the other triune identities, is not yet such a person. God is indeed describable as personal in the modern sense, but it is the triune event of which this is true, not the Father merely as Father. The person *that is* conscious is the Trinity. The Trinity is constituted a centered and possibly faithful self-consciousness by his object-reality as Jesus, the Son.

Indeed, neither the Father nor the Spirit can appropriately be grasped as an individual something, of the personal sort or any other. Jesus, who is the Son, is an individual personal thing; and the personal reality of God necessarily includes this fact, since only an individual something can be an object, here, God's Self as his Object. But—as we have insisted—it is *Jesus*, not a supernatural entity, an unincarnate Logos, that is this second and objective identity of God. And we must not now inflict on the Father or the Spirit the same sort of hypostasized supernatural reality from which we have just cleared the Son. Rather, we must press the doctrine that the triune identities are *relations* and say: What there is to being God the Father is being addressed as "Father" by the Son, Jesus; what there is to being God the Spirit is being the spirit of this communication. *In that* Jesus cries, "Father, into your hands . . . " and *in that* he who says this will be the final event, *there is* the Father. *In that* Jesus gives his spirit, and *in that* this gift will constitute the final community, *there is* the Spirit. This does not mean that Jesus creates the Father and the Spirit. As an individual person, he is one of the terms indeed necessarily posited for these as for any relations, but relations are not therefore secondary to their terms. And finally, *in that* all the above is true, Jesus *is* the Son.

It is also time to note and affirm a peculiarity of the meta-physical discourse now afoot. I have regularly been making metaphysical propositions that essentially include the proper name "Jesus" and solving metaphysical problems by reference to the historic reality of the particular person of that name. This violates the entire tradition, which presumes that meta-physical knowledge is attained—if at all—by a mode of gen-eralization that eliminates all such particular references;[25] thus, for example, Paul Tillich's problematic is constructed by a sup-posed tension between "ontological" and personal-religious ways of grasping reality.[26]

The historically great attempt to compromise the division was Hegel's, and his compromise's failure to convince ended the great creative surge of Western thought. Hegel, obeying the approved rule, generalized his trinitarianism, making the universe God's Object, "the Son," rather than the mere indi-vidual Jesus. But then he tried to remain Christian by saying that universal history could not in fact so function without containing some such historical appearance as Jesus[27]—to which everyone said, "Why not?"

But although the no-persons rule is primeval in our tradition, it is not therefore true or even intrinsically plausible. It is in fact merely a key assertion of one particular metaphysics, the very one against which trinitarianism has millennially strug-gled and which I have hoped again to attack. I assert that the particular historic reality of Jesus of Nazareth is the key func-tion in the true metaphysical structure of reality. Why not?

I conclude this section with a summary. The temporal infin-ity that opens before us and so surrounds us is the inexhaust-ibility of one event, the final appropriation of all history by the particular love actual as Jesus of Nazareth. In this recursive structure of the event, and given its particular content, the appropriation is an intended event, and its infinity that of consciousness.

God as Event

In a reality of which such propositions as those of the pre-vious section can be true, time does not work as the tradition has taught us. If time is either "linear" or "cyclical," if it either goes on and on by itself or is curved around in a third temporal mode—space—by a hidden motionless center, then to be real must be to *persist,* and then all realities must be substances, temporally extended somethings self-identical through their temporal extension by what they remain. Or, if events or ideas or whatever else are acknowledged real, their reality must be credited to their being acts, ideas, or whatevers *of* substance. But if time's essential mode, futurity, is infinite in the way just stipulated, then time is neither "linear" nor "cyclical," and therefore enduring realities need not be substances.

Wolfhart Pannenberg has proposed that we might conceive the Eschaton as a "contortion of time," a replacement of the temporal process as we know it by a different process, "a process into the depths of our present lives."[28] This is surely on the right line, except that "contortion" suggests that time is penultimately indeed linear or cyclical. Rather, since it is the oncoming of the future that *is* time, since it is the reality of the future that temporalizes us, the structure of the future, of the Eschaton if there is one, determines the character of time *as such.* If the Eschaton is as I have said, time is "now" neither merely lineal nor cyclical, and if we suppose it so, this is merely our error.

The future whose oncoming temporalizes us is an appropriation to each other of the specific event of Jesus and all created history. Therefore the very process of time is in fact a reaching *back* in *anticipation,* "a process into the depths of our present lives." Past and future do cohere for us despite everything. They do not cohere because some third fact (e.g., a timeless present) bridges the gap. They cohere because the future that is before us is the *interpreting* of all prior occurrence—of all that is then or at any penultimate time past—by a specific temporal occurrence. And the very specificity of this occurrence—love— is such that the interpreting is inexhaustible.

Thus if we posit, as we must, that there are enduring entities, then that any one moment in the history of such an entity *is* in the history of that entity (i.e., that it is "the same" entity as a past series of such moments) is not given by a mysterious persistence of those past moments. It is given by the unique interpretation to come, of the new moment together with the past moments, by the one particular event Jesus. In the case where the enduring entity is a conscious entity, the new moment is one life with a specific series of past moments not by memory but by hope, by vision of the unique meaning which the triumph of Jesus will give to just the series of this new moment and the previous moments. Therefore an enduring entity is at any moment *an* entity by structural openness to the future and is the *same* entity as itself in the future moment by the identity of that future.

But that is to say that enduring entities have the very structure which we are accustomed to attribute by speaking of an "event." If reality is as I have described it, "event" and "enduring entity" are not antithetical concepts, so that, leaping to our present main point, to call God an event is not to disqualify him as an enduring subject of actions and bearer of characteristics, but may be precisely to qualify him in these capacities. An "enduring entity" is simply an event in respect of its being analyzable into a series of events, each of which is in turn so analyzable, and so on. And an "event" is an enduring entity, seen in respect of its being a member of the history of a larger enduring entity, which in turn can be so seen, and so on. There must still be ontologically significant differences between at least two classes of enduring events[29] (e.g., a kiss, however prolonged, and a table); working that out is, however, beyond the scope of this book.

That God is both event and enduring entity, and that this can be so with him because it is so with anyone or anything, does not mean that he is event in the same way that we or other creatures are. I cohere as an event by virtue of a future event, the triumph of Jesus; I am not myself that event. God coheres as an event by virtue of a future event, the triumph of Jesus; he, however, is himself that event. Thus the event as which and the event by which God coheres are the same; that is, God is a triune event, which I am not.

To be sure, insofar as it is by God's triunity that he is personal, and insofar as I too am personal, there indeed obtain the analogies which Augustine discovered: my personhood is constituted in the dialectics of consciousness, objectivity, and spirit, as is God's by the dialectics of Father, Son, and Spirit. But what the analogies discover is my *personhood*, not triunity; they do not, as Augustine thought, reveal God's triunity or give meaning to trinitarian language about him. The analogies do not mean that I am *triune* or even analogously triune, only that I am personal. God is a triune and therefore eschatologically independent person. I am a merely singular, though complex, and therefore eschatologically dependent person.

Since personhood, in my interpretation, depends on the centering of consciousness over against an object other than the self, the identity of the event as which God is with the event by which he is would collapse God's personhood, save for the particular character of Jesus: that he is the person for others. God is his own *other*, to be independently *personal*, in that this other is in himself a person for other persons that God is not. This poses a question we have encountered before: Could then God have been the God he is had there been no such other persons, no creatures or no rescue of the fallen creatures? And the answer is also the same as before: The dialectics of deity, as I have described them, equally compel us to say that he could, that God is independently personal, and that we cannot know how. As it in fact is, his personhood is not posited apart from us, and we cannot cognitively transcend this fact. Some readers may think this result must show that my interpretation of deity is wrong. I can only ask them to reflect whether the contrary may not be the case.

Finally, I must note that the intent to interpret God's reality as event is by no means original with me. In fact, it is endemic in contemporary theology. Two major projects of twentieth-century theology have been largely devoted to carrying it out: that of Karl Barth's *Church Dogmatics* and that of "process" theology.

Barth is led to expound God's being as event by much the same consequences of trinitarianism that have led this book.[30] Initiating all interpretation of God with a trinitarian identification of him, Barth is freed from the tradition's prescription of the Hellenic identification and so is able to say, "God's deity consists, into its farthest depths, therein—or at least also therein—that it is event." Moreover, God's being is not event-hood, or something of that sort, but a particular event, "that event of God's activity in which we are involved in his reve-lation," the active relation of the triune persons.[31] Barth's doc-trine of God's being as love and freedom is then the explication of this being-as-event.[32] To the extent that theology currently tends to ignore the main parts of Barth's work, and in English-speaking territories has never grasped them, it has cut itself off from the main fully-realized attempt thus far to fulfill its own constant demand.

But an ambiguity pervades the *Church Dogmatics* at this very point, for Barth locates Christ's function as God's centering object not in Christ's final reality but in his primal reality. The eternity constituted between Christ and his Father is *"before* all time" and only so "after all time." It is in that God *pre*destines Jesus that Jesus is real in the prevenient divine life, to be the second instance of that life.[33] Thus Barth's "becoming" con-stantly threatens to appear as the persistence of the past after all, in spite of his stated intentions.[34] Despite the obvious great debt of the present work to Barth, my proposals have been and must be very different from his at most key points.

"Process" theology is perhaps the most influential single school in contemporary English-speaking theology. It is there-fore the more regrettable that this theology is often thought to specify God's being as event and in fact does not, thereby spreading endless confusion. Just so, I must devote some space to the matter. I will not denote by "process theology" all the-ology that has learned from Whitehead or Hartshorne (that would be almost all English-language theology), but only those theologies that find in these philosophers "the right philoso-phy" and so maintain the key doctrines of their interpretation of God.[35] Thus my own citations will be from Hartshorne himself.[36]

It is true that "process" metaphysics understands all reality as concretely consisting in events, and so also God as so consisting. What there most concretely is, is in no case a substance (e.g., "this man") but the momentary events of the man's life. The enduring entity, "this man," is then a series of events established as an identifiable series by certain kinds of likeness and other relations between the events.[37]

Thus no enduring entity is, in this metaphysics, itself an event, but rather a certain sort of abstraction from some set of events. *Neither then is God.* But whereas each human or each galaxy or indeed each enduring entity other than God is an abstraction from its own specifiable set of events—so that it makes sense to say, for example, that this human *is* such-and-such events—the events that God concretely is are simply all the events that are the history of the world. Therefore, if our discourse remains at the concrete level, that is, at the level of event-discourse, the word "God" has no import of its own and we cannot with it denote any identifiable reality. Concretely (i.e., as *event!*) there is only the world. There is God as "God," as more than the world, only in God's "*abstract* character," in that kind of his reality that is grasped by abstraction from concrete reality, that is, from talking about "events." God is in this analysis not an event but an in itself timelessly given structure of relations between all events. "Process" metaphysics may— and in my opinion does—contribute greatly to our understanding of the general character of reality, but as exposition of the assertion "God is event" it contributes nothing whatever, having never taken up the question. "Process" metaphysics demotes the notion of substance. But once we do come to speak of the enduring entities to which the notion was applied— whether an amoeba or God—they continue to assume it, and with all its traditional determinants.

Being

So what is it to be? The great ontological question must be my last question, even though within the scope of this book I can touch it only aphoristically. What do we know about x when all we know is that x IS x? What is being?

In a Christian reflection, the question is answered by seeking

determinants that can be switched to state the difference between the Creator and his creatures, and then using them indifferently to the switch.[38] Thus in traditional doctrine a standard evocation of being is: To be God is to be the Explanation;
to be a creature is to require explanation; *ens est veritas*. It is not
to be expected that any one such set of propositions is the
single most appropriate, which does not mean that some are
not true and others false, or even that some true sets are not
more appropriate than others. I here offer the following, in less
concise form than I would wish.

To be God is to anticipate a future self by an inexhaustible
interpretive relation to an other that God himself is; to be a
creature is to anticipate a future self, by a finite interpretive
relation to an other that the creature is not; being is interpretive
relatedness across time. Had this book a different scope, the
next urgent task would be to show how this interpretation can
fit beings other than persons. Instead, I will be yet more violently aphoristic and say, Being is interpretive relatedness
across time; that is, to be is to rise from the dead. Such is the
description of reality that coheres with trinitarian doctrine of
God.

NOTES

1. Gregory of Nyssa *To Ablabius: That There Are Not Three Gods*, in
his *Opera*, vol. 3/1, ed. F. Müller (Leiden: Brill, 1958), p. 42.

2. So, e.g., Thomas Aquinas; see Robert W. Jenson, *The Knowledge of Things Hoped For* (New York: Oxford University Press, 1969),
pp. 58ff.

3. On the theological use of "infinite" prior to Gregory, and on
Gregory's originality, see Ekkehard Mühlenberg, *Die Unendlichkeit
Gottes bei Gregor von Nyssa* (Göttingen: Vandenhoeck & Ruprecht,
1966), pp. 63–82.

4. Aristotle *Physics* 207a1.

5. Aristotle *On the Generations of Animals* 1.

6. To the following, see Mühlenberg, *Unendlichkeit*, pp. 29–58.

7. E.g., Aristotle *Posterior Analytics* 836.5.

8. Mühlenberg, *Unendlichkeit*, e.g., pp. 165ff.

9. For a surplus of citations, ibid., esp. pp. 106–11.

10. Gregory of Nyssa *Against Eunomius* in his *Opera*, vols. 1–2, ed. W. Jaeger (Leiden: Brill, 1960), 1:366.

11. Ibid., 2:69–70. General proof of this point may be left to Mühlenberg, *Unendlichkeit*, whose chief general thesis this is.

12. As Mühlenberg, ibid., esp. pp. 100–147, has surely established, Gregory uses "infinite" precisely in the sense defined by Aristotle, of that which provokes a regress to infinity in our reasoning. Just so, Aristotle's God is not infinite and Gregory's is.

13. Cf. Jean Daniélou, *L'être et le temps chez Grégoire de Nysse* (Leiden: Brill, 1970), esp. pp. 95–115.

14. Gregory of Nyssa *Eunomius* 3/10:36.

15. Ibid., 1.666–72.

16. Friedrich Nietzsche, *Werke* (Munich: Hansen Verlag, 1955), 3:125.

17. This is the heart of the earlier much-discussed phenomenon of secularization, of which Friedrich Gogarten, *Der Mensch Zwischen Gott und Welt* (Stuttgart: Friedrich Vorwerk, 1956), and *Verhängnis und Hoffnung der Neuzeit* (Stuttgart: Friedrich Vorwerk, 1959), is still the most powerful theological analyst.

18. E.g., Karl Jaspers, *Man in the Modern Age*, trans. E. and C. Paul (London: Routledge & Kegan Paul, 1951).

19. Impressed on a whole generation of theologians by Oscar Cullmann, *Christ and Time*, trans. F. V. Filson (Philadelphia: Westminster, 1950).

20. Rudolf Bultmann, "Der christliche Hoffnung und das Problem der Entmythologisierung," in his *Glauben und Verstehen* (Tübingen: J. C. B. Mohr, 1962), 3:81–90; "Geschichte und Eschatologie im Neuen Testament," ibid., pp. 91–106.

21. E.g., "A Theological Conversation with Wolfhart Pannenberg," *Dialog* 11 (1972): 287–88.

22. This is one way of locating the point where Hegel's synthesis collapsed. The only way in which consciousness might be interpreted as substance is if it is understood as essentially and independently *self*-consciousness, so that the object by which it achieves reality is merely itself. This self-consciousness must be "immediate," not initially mediated by other consciousnesses; I must be conscious of my self whether or not I have as my object another consciousness that has me for its object. But just so, the biblical apprehension of the contingent object is in fact suppressed, and appears in the system only as an accusatory and finally malignant memory.

23. Jean-Paul Sartre, *L'être et le Néant* (Paris: Gallimard, 1943).

24. Karl Barth, *Kirchliche Dogmatik* (Zurich: Zollikon, 1932–67), 4/3:202.

25. E.g., Gotthold Lessing's famous dictum in *On Demonstration in Spirit and Power* (1717): "Accidental historical truths can never be the proof of necessary truths of reason."

26. Paul Tillich, *Biblical Religion and the Search for Ultimate Reality* (Chicago: University of Chicago Press, 1955).

27. See the fine account in Emanuel Hirsch, *Geschichte der neuern evangelischen Theologie* (Gütersloh: Bertelsmann, 1954), 5:253–60.

28. "Theological Conversation with Pannenberg," pp. 287–88.

29. Classic here is P. F. Strawson, *Individuals* (London: Methuen, 1950).

30. Barth, *Dogmatik*, 2/1:288–305.

31. Ibid., pp. 284, 300.

32. Ibid., pp. 306–34, 334–61. Colin Gunton, *Becoming and Being* (Oxford: Oxford University Press, 1978), pp. 17–214; Robert W. Jenson, *God after God* (Indianapolis: Bobbs-Merrill, 1969).

33. Robert W. Jenson, *Alpha and Omega* (New York: Nelson, 1963), pp. 65ff., 141.

34. Critique of Barth at this point, including my own published critique, is neatly summarized and evaluated by Gunton, *Becoming*, pp. 177–85.

35. E.g., John Cobb, *A Christian Natural Theology* (London: Lutterworth, 1966); Ralph E. James, *The Concrete God* (Indianapolis: Bobbs-Merrill, 1967); Schubert Odgen, *The Reality of God* (New York: Harper & Row, 1966).

36. Dependent on Gunton, *Becoming*, pp. 11–114.

37. To this paragraph, e.g., Charles Hartshorne, *A Natural Theology for Our Time* (LaSalle: Open Court, 1967), pp. 6–28; *The Divine Relativity* (New Haven: Yale University Press, 1948), pp. 3–47, 67–75, 88–94. An impression of the utter opposition of Hartshorne's interpretation of God to that presented here can be gleaned from such passages as *Man's Vision of God* (Chicago: Willett, Clark, 1941), pp. 251ff.; *Natural Theology*, p. 101.

38. One may or may not acquiesce in calling this procedure "analogy." The procedure to which the term is historically attached shares the features stated here but incorporates others of which I cannot approve; see Jenson, *Knowledge*, pp. 58–98.

Afterword

We have covered much territory, historically and systematically. One thing makes this book's various historical expositions and proclamatory and speculative proposals a continuous argument: concern for the identification of God. If this is kept in mind, the lines between chapters and sections of chapters can be drawn crisscross at will. For example, the metaphysical proposals of the last chapter may be described as analyses of the sort of reality whose God can have, as in Chapter 1, a proper name; or the biblical exegesis of Chapter 2 may be taken as the Scripture proofs for the dogma described in Chapter 3, and so on.

Though "identity" is not a key word in the tradition before Barth, the concern it names is anything but novel. The bulk and difficulty of the deposited tradition that I have had to mediate and explain testify to the extraordinary concentration and labor which the church's thought, in its lively periods, has devoted to the matters I find it helpful to caption "identity." And even so, I have selected ruthlessly and after the year 451 have reported only the western European tradition. But in the Western church's current state of piety and thought, concern for the particular identity of the gospel's God must nevertheless appear eccentric, and in ways, I, before actually displaying the trinitarian oddities and offenses, could in Chapter 1 only suggest.

Thus the very chapter titles of this book must be a mere set of outrages to late twentieth-century bureaucratic and solipistic civilization and to a church that has capitulated to it. That God has some proper name, never mind this one, means among other things that not all addresses to deity are equally true, that it is possible to be in simple error at the very base of religious life. What free white American, taste-testing the religious smorgasbord for the offerings that make him feel best about himself, will tolerate such a notion? That Christian experience has a definite logical structure means that Christian discourse and work present something to study, learn, practice, and speculate upon. What seminary faculty, arranging experiences and setting skill outcomes for the students, has time for such a reactionary attitude? That there are any dogmas at all, much less the drastically particularizing dogma of Nicaea and Constantinople, means among other things that there must be church discipline. What bishop, ordaining his annual crop of Buddhists and Mother-Goddess cultists, wants to think about that? And as for the elaborate and profound matters of developed trinitarian doctrine and metaphysics, those in our society and church sufficiently well educated to deal with such matters are ever more a small and circumscribed elite; the rest are merely offended that there should be any discussions so far beyond their grasp.

Yet trinitarianism, if radical enough, is also desperately contemporary, for it is the positive of that biblical interpretation of God that in its negative power has broken the Hellenic securities and created our infinitely threatened world. It is the positive of that grasp of reality which in its unbelieving form is the source of the churchly and civil philistinisms just lamented. The whole of this book can indeed be read as a sustained argument for the proposition that consistently trinitarian faith is now the West's only open alternative to nihilism.

Whether the Western church can renew its trinitarianism, whether it can recover specifically Christian proclamation and faith, may well be doubted. A newly Christian church would be very much smaller than the present phenomenon; whether the presence of such a small sect would suffice to counter the nihilistic impulse in our civilization may also be doubted. But on both counts it is surely worth trying.

If it should turn out that trinitarianism has definitely ceased in the West, the gospel will nevertheless continue elsewhere, and so will the gospel's interpreting of God. In the life and reflection of the African and Asian churches, the immediate trinitarianism described in Chapters 1 and 2 plays and will play much the same role as in the story we have told. The developed reflection of the remaining chapters, dependent as it is on the particular partner which our culture-religion sets for the gospel, will not be reproduced in other branches of the gospel's history. But analogues must surely appear. Perhaps in the struggle for and about these, the Western church's trinitarian history, including such efforts as we now make, could—even in the worst case of their own vitality—play a final exemplary and cautionary role.

It all has to do, after all, with the simplest of mysteries: that we may in God's own Spirit approach him as Father, because we do so with the man Jesus. Or, that our times cohere not because their differences are unreal but because the relations between them are enacted in the one man Jesus' life and in his resurrection.

Indexes

SUBJECTS

189

PERSONS